HEART HAPPY

Heart Happy

Staying Centered in God's Love through Chaotic Circumstances

Tricia Goyer

SALEM
BOOKS
an imprint of Regnery Publishing
Washington, D.C.

Salem Books™ is a trademark of Salem Communications Holding Corporation. Regnery® is a registered trademark and its colophon is a trademark of Salem Communications Holding Corporation.

ISBN: 978-1-68451-163-1
eISBN: 978-1-68451-208-9

Library of Congress Control Number: 2021946361

Published in the United States by
Salem Books
An Imprint of Regnery Publishing
A Division of Salem Media Group
Washington, D.C.
www.SalemBooks.com

Manufactured in the United States of America

10 9 8 7 6 5 4 3 2 1

Books are available in quantity for promotional or premium use. For information on discounts and terms, please visit our website: www.SalemBooks.com

"*Heart Happy* is the book I didn't know I needed, but so desperately did. The way Tricia Goyer weaves her personal life experiences with the truth of God will touch women in every phase and stage of life, guiding them gently to find their own heart happiness that has become buried under the responsibilities and chaos of life. She shares her own struggles with unflinching honesty and confidence that clearly come from her relationship with Christ, along with practical steps to grow closer to God in meaningful and lasting ways. This is a must-read for every woman yearning to find innate joy and abiding happiness in a world that makes both hard to find."

—**Jen Babakhan**, author of *Detoured: The Messy, Grace-Filled Journey From Working Professional to Stay-at-Home Mom*

"*Heart Happy* is filled with honesty and hope. From her own difficult experiences, Tricia Goyer shares how she's drawn closer to God in the midst of chaos and learned to nurture her soul in His presence. I found so much wisdom within these pages and will return to them again. Highly recommended."

—**Robin Lee Hatcher**, Christy Award–winning author of eighty-five books, including *I'll Be Seeing You*

"I resonated so much with Tricia's honesty and her battle with being kind to herself. Her reliance on Scripture, the well-told stories, and quotes from past saints helped me reorient my heart toward finally believing my heart is worth caring for. If you're frazzled, beaten down by life, or just plain weary, *Heart Happy* will do just that—help your heart to find peaceful happiness, even in the midst of chaos and stress."

—**Mary DeMuth**, author of *The Most Misunderstood Women of the Bible*

"With her trademark candor and real-life stories, Tricia shows us that it's possible to grow and even thrive during a difficult season. This book will point you back to what really matters and plant seeds of hope and cheer in your heart."

—**Robin Jones Gunn**, bestselling author of *Victim of Grace* and 100 other books, including the *Christy Miller* series

"Tricia Goyer speaks right to the heart of women who long for contentment. Warm, transparent, and weighted in practical application of biblical truths, *Heart Happy* helps us rise above chaos to embrace joy in the Lord. I highly recommend this gem of a book!"

—**Ginger Hubbard**, bestselling author of *Don't Make Me Count to Three* and co-host of the *Parenting with Ginger Hubbard* podcast

"Searching for goodness and happiness is something we all long for deep in our souls. If you are looking for a biblically based approach to happiness, then *Heart Happy* is for you. Tricia is a trustworthy guide to lead you to find rest, peace, and happiness while living in the middle of the storm."

—**Sarah Bragg**, author of *A Mother's Guide to Raising Herself*

"As I work with clients in the counseling office constantly struggling to hold on to joy in the midst of suffering, I have always wished there were a book I could give them to encourage them along the way. *Heart Happy* offers powerful truth along with compassionate care that I believe will encourage the soul in the midst of darkness moving towards the light of hope again."

—**Michelle Nietert**, host of the *Raising Mentally Healthy Kids* podcast and author of *Loved and Cherished* and *Make Up Your Mind*

"What a beautiful, timely reminder that living with a happy heart is within reach for all of us. Tricia Goyer has anchored herself to God's love and hope in the middle of chaos. She writes as a faithful friend to help us do the same. This book won't weigh you down with more to do. Instead, it will liberate you to live in freedom, ready to experience the mercies of God each day."

—**Arlene Pellicane**, speaker, host of the *Happy Home* podcast, and author of *31 Days to Becoming a Happy Mom*

"*Heart Happy* is the exhale you've been longing for. With candor, Tricia Goyer shares some of her deepest wounds and darkest days in order to show how God can create a happy heart even in the midst of so much hurt and chaos. For whatever reason, Christian culture has deemed joy more holy than happiness. Armed with the Truth of God's Word and some simple soul care practices, Tricia shows us how we can have both."

—**Jamie Erickson**, author of *Homeschool Bravely: How to Squash Doubt, Trust God, and Teach Your Child with Confidence* and co-host of the *Mom to Mom* podcast

"Life is loud, isn't it? Do you believe God longs for your heart to be happy in Him in the midst of all the noise? Because He does, and we can be so, no matter the decibel of distraction or discouragement we experience! Even though we have access to more apps on our phones and to more people and information than ever before—happiness feels fleeting, doesn't it? This is because access to more comes with the temptation and pressure to do and be more! Similar to Tricia Goyer, I've learned that access to more usually ends up producing more chaos instead of calm in my heart and mind. As a result, my happiness decreases, and I bet the same is true for you. Which is why I am grateful for this book! Author Tricia Goyer will encourage you throughout the following pages if you are longing for some heart happiness to hold you as you face the stresses and hurts in your life. You will be encouraged as she shows you how to securely live in the center of God's embrace whenever more of anything tries to hinder your happiness."

—**Tracy Steel**, mentor, speaker, and author of *A Redesigned Life: Uncovering God's Purpose When Life Doesn't Go As Planned*

"I've read a lot about, and even written about, prioritizing our relationship with God over religious rituals. In the context of Tricia's profoundly important understanding of happiness, I'm even more inspired to do this. If we think happiness is based on our circumstances or is something we must have and can create for ourselves, we often make unhealthy and unwise decisions. It can be a dangerous pursuit. Understanding that happiness is not emotional—it's positional, it's what God wants for us—will change us! Tricia's relatable illustrations, relevant truths, and practical ideas will free you and empower you to successfully and joyfully pursue God and experience the depth of His love!"

—**Dr. Kathy Koch**, founder of Celebrate Kids, Inc. and author of *8 Great Smarts, Start with the Heart, Screens and Teens,* and *Five to Thrive*

Jesus, thank You. I love You, too.

CONTENTS

INTRODUCTION
Made New: Remembering What God Has Done   xiii

CHAPTER ONE
Heart Happy: Connection through Honest Confession   1

CHAPTER TWO
Life's Chaos, God's Embrace: The Secret of Surrender   13

CHAPTER THREE
The Priority of a Happy Heart: Receiving God's Love   23

CHAPTER FOUR
The Sensitivity of God, the Sovereignty of God:
Surrender and Trust   43

CHAPTER FIVE
Let's Talk about a Happy Heart: Defeating Shame   63

CHAPTER SIX
Scripture Nourishment, Prayer, and Listening to
God's Voice: The Power of Prayer   83

CHAPTER SEVEN
Worthy, Not Abandoned: Understanding Your Value   105

CHAPTER EIGHT
Being Compassionate to Others and Ourselves:
Accepting True Grace   127

CHAPTER NINE
Soul Care in the Midst of Suffering and Pain: Resilience   **141**

CHAPTER TEN
**Finding Your Creative Refuge: The Steadfast Shelter
of God**   **159**

Notes   **179**

Made New
Remembering What God Has Done

For once you were full of darkness,
but now you have light from the Lord.
So live as people of light!

Ephesians 5:8

I t was an ordinary moment in 1989, until it wasn't. Well, as ordinary as it could be for a high school dropout, seventeen and pregnant. It was nearly noon when I awoke, and my expanding waistline forced me to flop as I curled to my side. Deep-pitted depression and feelings of hopelessness cocooned me like a suffocating blanket. Bright light shone through the high bedroom window, but inside I felt only darkness.

What have I done with my life? My boyfriend had moved on. Friends, too. Cheerleading uniforms hung in my closet with no chance of fitting now. Miles away, the rest of Weed (California) High School's class of 1989 prepped for the prom. The most excitement I'd had in recent days was ordering receiving blankets from a JCPenney catalog.

This isn't how life was supposed to turn out. What's going to happen to me? How can I care for my baby? What am I going to do with my life?

My life.

That was the problem: I'd claimed my life as my own. Even though my mom and I had regularly attended church since I was in the second grade, by high school, I'd chosen my own path rather than the ways I'd been taught. Longing for love, I'd looked to boys. I ended up pregnant and alone. Yet as I lay there, I considered the words to my favorite Sunday School song.

Jesus loves me, this I know … The words played over and over in my mind.

Did He Love Me? Could He?

It seemed impossible, really. I'd pushed every thought of a loving God out of my mind as I'd pursued popularity and pleasure. *Does He love me … even now?* The answer, I knew, could change everything.

My mind flipped between reality and hope. I'd really messed up. Not only was I pregnant at seventeen, but I'd also had an abortion two years prior. Yet hope dared to believe God's love remained.

Wondering if God still cared despite my mistakes, I considered my mom's church friends. Her Bible study group had invited me to join them, and they planned a baby shower. The pastor's wife had come to our house to visit me and pray. *Maybe if those ladies love me, God loves me, too.*

Even as darkness pressed down, I tilted my chin toward Heaven, and the softest whisper escaped my lips: "God, I have screwed up big-time. If You could do anything with my life, please do."

It wasn't the most eloquent prayer, but in an instant, over-bearing darkness became light. Where there'd been despair, hope appeared. Joy expelled the sadness, loneliness, and fear with a hefty shove. More than joy, happiness descended, too. Knowing that Jesus loved me and had good plans for my life changed everything. That simple confession changed my life.

For months I lived *heart happy*, knowing I'd been given a second chance. Three months later, my son Cory was born. This handsome baby was a gift from God—true beauty after the pain of my past mistakes.

After my first prayer, I had dared to whisper a second: "God, could You bring me someone to love me and love my baby?" And God answered that one, too. John Goyer—the pastor's son—came into my life. We married when Cory was nine months old, and in four years, we had two more children. We attended church and became involved in Bible studies.

Though I initially realized I'd get nowhere in life without God, the rituals of being a good Christian mom (and later wife) took my focus. I strove to live right and "make it up to" God for my mistakes. Nowhere in the Bible are we told to do this. In fact, it says the opposite.

First John 1:9 says, "But if we confess our sins to him, he is faithful and just to forgive us our sins and to cleanse us from all wickedness." I knew this with my mind, but I didn't feel it.

The guilt of the abortion I'd had when I was fifteen weighed on my chest like a heavy boulder. I told no one. Only my old boyfriend, my mom, and John knew. I feared my friends would hate me if they found out.

I believed God loved me, but my sin seemed too big to release. Instead of letting go, I attempted to make up for my past mistakes.

Joy took a backseat to serving God. And happiness? Well, it seemed wrong to desire it. I still loved God, but I'd forgotten the true happiness that came the moment I dumped my mess onto Jesus's lap and asked Him to do something with it. Yes, even the best moments become memories, and life resumes. Somewhere along the way, devotion became duty. Can you relate? Wanting to prove to God, myself, and others that I was more than the sum of my past mistakes, I longed to make a difference in this world. Busyness became my banner. If ever someone rushed to please God, it was me.

In my twenties and thirties, I became a Christian writer and speaker. I helped launch a crisis pregnancy center. I homeschooled my kids and led a support group for teen moms. In my thirties and forties, my husband and I adopted seven children (after raising our three to adulthood).

As the years passed, I found healing from the pain and shame of my former sins. I'd even dared to believe God forgave every sin—even the sin of abortion. Still, the habit of hurriedness ruled my routines. Adding lots of kids to an already-busy life doesn't work, at least not well. I knew things had to change, so I started cutting out a lot.

But when I chose to slow down, the drama in my home escalated. Parenting kids who'd faced past trauma was more challenging than I ever dreamed. All my "tools" of being a good mom failed...and sometimes they even made matters worse. (Did you know that having someone love you can be scary for a child who's faced past trauma? It can.)

After attempting to parent challenging children (amid everything else), I found the end of myself, my abilities, and even my happiness. My happy heart lay hidden, buried under duty and responsibility. Secondary trauma shrouded my heart with a layer of pain. Things needed to change. Busyness + hurting kids and hurting parents = chaos. That little word represents a lot, doesn't it? Chaos had hung around the outskirts of life for years—decades, even. But as we added children into our home, chaos staked a claim and advanced into every part of my life.

That's how my search for heart happiness really began. In the pages ahead, I'll tell you how I found it through and amidst the chaos.

Where God's Love Fits In

I've spent many paragraphs sharing my journey out of darkness into light, from heartache to happiness, and from contrition to chaos. Perhaps your story has similar elements, or maybe it's completely different, but you still find yourself overwhelmed, out of sorts, and overloaded. You've been trying everything to fix the feelings of failure that flood your mind: You're not doing this right...something's wrong. Yet the fix eludes you. Everything you've tried has fallen short. I understand. I've been there, too.

The good news is there is an answer, and the solution won't add any line items to your to-do list—not even one. The key to being heart happy (which we all long for!) has nothing to do with what *you* need to do. Instead, it's all about remembering (again and again) what *God* has done.

Staying centered in God's love through chaotic circumstances is key to everything. It's looking up to God's loving gaze before looking around at the mess we're in. It's allowing our hearts to be filled with God's love, even when we feel like failures.

Being centered in God's love has changed me. I will state right now that the chaotic circumstances of my life have not changed much in the last two years. As you will read within the pages of this book, they've gotten worse. In fact, if I were to try to put all the circumstances John and I have walked through into a novel, I would have to cut some of them out. Even in the best pieces of fiction, there comes the point where the reader says, "Okay, enough conflict, let's move to the happy ending, please." There have been many days when I've wished for the same. Though I'm skilled at scripting novels, I can't script my life. So far, the silver lining is still far out of view. And that's why I wanted to write this book now, for you—and for myself, too.

I'm writing in the middle of the maelstrom. If I've learned to cultivate a happy heart during storms and squalls, heartaches and hardships, you can too. Even though I'm using the word "cultivation," know the answer isn't found in anything you or I need to do. Instead, God has already provided His love in multiple ways, and it's available to us anytime. The answer is in truly understanding that and living as if we are completely loved. It's easy—and it's not. It's easy because God's love is always available. It's not, because there are hundreds of things that keep us from fully surrendering to it. I'll talk all about that in these pages.

This book is about centering ourselves in God's love and allowing the life we live to pour out from it. It's believing heart happy is possible—even here, even now, even today. Climbing into God's embrace in the middle of our chaos can change everything, and I don't say that lightly. I'm able to sit down and write words of hope because I've experienced hope deep in my soul. Now, I want to give you the same.

"Heart Happy" might seem like an ungodly term, and that's why I'm so excited about this book. What would you say if I told you that God longs for our hearts to be happy in Him? Would you believe our hearts were made for happiness in the Lord? Could you accept that it's possible even in the most challenging circumstances that life throws at us? They were, and it is.

There's nothing revolutionary about what I share on these pages. My guess is that you've read and heard lots of messages about being centered on God's love. I hope this one will be more than just ideas you file away, but rather habits you embrace— practices that stem from desire, not duty. Patterns that foster soul care, rather than just fabricating more things to feel insufficient about.

At the end of each chapter, I've provided one practical—yet simple—takeaway. These aren't more things to add to your to-do list. In fact, these takeaways have very little to do with "doing." Instead, they have more to do with what we choose to believe.

Heart happiness is rooted in understanding God's love and embracing it daily. Instead of checking off items on a to-do list, heart happiness is about going to God to seek His tender mercies again and again. As I sit here, a little bit overwhelmed and even more tired, my soul sings. Heart happiness is a discovery that has changed me from the inside out, and I can't wait to share it with you. Ready to begin?

CHAPTER ONE

Heart Happy
Connection through Honest Confession

Watch over your heart with all diligence,
For from it flow the springs of life.

Proverbs 4:23 NASB

One of my Christian heroes is George Müller. George and his wife felt drawn to the plight of orphans in Bristol, England, and opened a home for thirty girls in 1836. Seeing a great need, Müller continued to open houses and through them, cared for more than ten thousand children in his lifetime. He also made it a point never to ask others to meet the orphans' needs. Instead, he took all their needs to God in prayer. Not receiving government support and only accepting unsolicited gifts, his organization received and disbursed £1,381,171 over Müller's lifetime (which would be more than $1.9 million today).[1] What an amazing testimony!

One of the most inspiring things to me about Müller is that all he did flowed out of a happy heart. On May 9, 1841, five years after he opened his first orphanage, he wrote:

It has pleased the Lord to teach me a truth, the benefit
of which I have not lost, for more than fourteen years.
The point is this: I saw more clearly than ever that the
first great and primary business to which I ought to
attend every day was to have my soul happy in the Lord.
The first thing to be concerned about was not how much
I might serve the Lord, or how I might glorify the Lord;
but how I might get my soul into a happy state, and how
my inner man might be nourished. For I might seek to
set the truth before the unconverted, I might seek to
benefit believers, I might seek to relieve the distressed, I
might in other ways seek to behave myself as it becomes
a child of God in this world; and yet, not being happy in
the Lord, and not being nourished and strengthened in
my inner man day by day, all this might not be attended
to in a right spirit.[2]

Nearly two hundred years ago, George Müller realized that our
most significant concern in life shouldn't be doing great things,
caring for others, or even serving and glorifying the Lord. All of
these are important. All can be achieved, but the external should
stem from the internal. Our outward actions should flow from the
wellspring of happiness found from God's love welling up within
us. Doing, caring, and serving in any other way simply leaves us
exhausted and won't carry us far.

George Müller 's priority can change everything if we make it
our priority, too. Getting our souls into a happy state so that our
inner man (or woman!) might be nourished infuses our tasks with
new life, new strength, and a new happiness. The abundance of
Müller's life flowed out of the abundance of his heart. What he

achieved is clearly seen, but his accomplishments were only possible because he took time to seek a heart happy in the Lord.

Happy Hearts Blossom into Thriving Lives

Only through happy hearts and nourished souls do we live thriving lives. Anything less is just going through the motions. No matter how motivated we are, we can't keep up good works through an empty soul for long. We can share the truth of God's Word with the lost, serve our families and community, help the hurting, and act with love and charity, but if we don't do these things from the outpouring of happy hearts, we'll feel purposeless and dry.

Have you ever felt that way? I have. And then I gave up. Either that, or I struggled on. I questioned if there was more to the Christian life than what I was experiencing. I went through the motions and shared how Jesus changes everything, but deep down, I didn't feel changed at all.

Without a soul nourished by the Lord, any season of trying to live "a life that really matters" will be a bright and shiny flash of inspiration that fizzles and dies. Unable to keep on keeping on, we'll fall back to dry and straightforward rituals that don't take much energy, like walking into a church service and leaving an hour later with a happy thought for the day. Or buying a devotional book and making it fifteen pages in before it ends up on the bookshelf alongside twenty more just like it.

We may have enough oomph to share Scripture graphics on our Facebook page and hope that someone will be inspired, but the messages fall far short of hitting our own hearts. We will tell others about God's love even though we don't really feel it ourselves. But what else can we do? We have no energy to make a real difference, and we feel disillusioned with the Christian life. Even if we don't walk away from faith in God, we may believe that only a passionate few are chosen to lead thriving, purposeful lives. Either that, or they're faking it.

Do you do any of the following things?

- Fall into simple and dry rituals that don't take energy
- Seek happy thoughts to buoy your spirit because you don't have the inspiration to do much more
- Have little energy to make a real difference
- Feel disillusioned with the Christian life
- Believe God only calls a passionate few to lead thriving, purposeful lives
- Think those who are exuberant for God are faking it

What if things don't have to be that way? What if, like Müller, you choose to start your day by getting your soul into a happy state so that your inner self might be nourished? What do you imagine could flourish from a nourished soul? The possibilities are endless!

Focusing on Happy Hearts

We don't have to fumble through the Christian life. We don't have to give up on doing good. Instead, it comes down to this: focusing on making our hearts happy first in the Lord, knowing everything good flows from that. From today on, let's focus on becoming heart happy. We can make soul nourishment a priority. We can have peace and strength. We can experience hope and joy, even during a busy life or demanding circumstances.

How can we make our hearts happy? My goal is to share many ideas, but the place to start is here: Spend time with God in His Word—not just to "learn" about, but to connect with God. Müller writes:

> I began therefore to meditate on the New Testament from the beginning, early in the morning. The first thing I did, after having asked in a few words the Lord's blessing upon his precious Word, was, to begin to meditate on the Word of God, searching as it were into every verse, to get blessing out of it; not for the sake of the public ministry of the Word, not for the sake of preaching on what I had meditated upon, but for the sake of obtaining food for my own soul.[3]

What would it be like to wake up tomorrow and spend five minutes reading God's Word, seeking whatever good news and blessing He has for your heart? How would things change? Don't just pass up these questions. Pause and think about them. How would things change? My guess is that they would change for the better. How do I know? I've experienced unbelievable changes, and I know you would too.

Most mornings, I'm awake before everyone in the house. With my husband, five kids still at home, and my grandma here, too, early mornings are my only quiet time. I read God's Word, and I find happiness in my moments with Him. I pray and settle my heart on Jesus. I turn my thoughts to His big plans for me, my family, and the world, and then I look at my to-do list in light of that. Only then can I bravely face the demands of my day.

As an author of more than eighty books, a speaker, podcast host, and homeschooling mom of ten children (and caregiver to my grandma!), people ask me how I do it all. The answer is this: I take time to nourish my soul. I get my heart happy and focused on God in numerous ways, and it's from that filled-up heart that I pour out. I tend to myself so I'll be able to tend to others.

For me, "tending" is knowing what needs to be done and making time to do it. According to Dictionary.com, "tending" means "to care for or look after; give one's attention to." When I started a (tiny!) garden last year, I made space and prepared the soil. I planted seeds and sprouts, and then every day from May to October, I watered and cared for those plants. It wasn't a ton of work, but it was daily…and that's the whole point. Tending is a daily act.

Don't worry, I'm not going to overuse the tending metaphor. I didn't break up the sections with titles such as "Preparing the Soil," "Weeding," "Watering," or "The Light of the Sun/Son." My goal isn't to expand a metaphor but to pull out this application: every small decision to tend your soul and to turn your heart to God WILL bring change. When you draw near to God first, you will make your heart happy in the Lord. Experiencing God in these moments will allow you to know and feel His love. As this happens, you become centered even in chaotic circumstances.

The Middle English root word for "tending" means "to move or be inclined to move in a certain direction." The goal here is not to perfectly practice soul care by forcing oneself to be happy in the Lord. I guarantee there's nothing perfect about my tending. Instead, the goal is to make positive changes to cultivate a happy heart.

Some ideas that I share are disciplines I've cultivated over the years. Others are new habits I've developed after thirty-one years of being a Christian. Recently, as I've turned to God in both straightforward and profound ways, my inner peace, joy, and happiness have multiplied exponentially. Despite that, life is far more complex and complicated now than it ever was. (Parenting ten children from ages ten to thirty-one will do that!)

Most days are organized chaos at best. But during these crazy days, I've discovered that there is beauty in chaos. Why? The commotion, mayhem, and pandemonium have catapulted me straight into God's embrace in new ways. There's nothing more wonderful than resting there, soaking in His love, and feeling His approval as I focus on the beating of my Lord's heart.

Yet, for many years, I couldn't imagine drawing close to God. Why? Mostly because I felt guilty and ashamed. While God longed to draw near to me, I often found myself pushing Him away. The thought of God drawing near brought fear and panic. I knew He'd see all my flaws. Like a child who stole cookies from the jar, I didn't want to be found out. Have you ever felt that way? The good news is that we don't have to carry that guilt. Instead, when we release all that's holding us back, we often discover what our souls have truly been longing for: our God who longs to draw close.

Going Deeper

A Happy Heart Starts with Confession

Guilt and shame…each of us faces these emotions. They are part of my story—a dark, depressing part. Maybe these emotions have plagued you in the past. Perhaps they still do. As you've probably figured out, trying to ignore complicated emotions gets us nowhere.

Emotions are signals that something is going on in our hearts. We often label them "bad" or "good," but every emotion reflects what is going on within us. Emotions such as guilt and shame are billboards telling us that we have fallen short of God's standards and need to make things right with Him. Complex emotions won't go away until we deal with the root of the pain.

Like me, you can go to Jesus and confess those sins. Confession that comes from a sorrowful and humble heart will be accepted by God. Psalm 51:17 says, "The sacrifice you desire is a broken spirit. You will not reject a broken and repentant heart, O God." When you confess, Jesus wipes away all your sins as if they never happened. He will not reject your brokenness. In fact, He welcomes you with open arms. But you must be willing to first confess—then accept you've been forgiven.

Years ago, one of my daughters started walking with a limp. At first, I thought she was simply trying to act silly. When I asked about it, she told me her foot had been bothering her. We looked at it a few times but didn't see anything wrong. Then, after some probing (literal probing), my husband found the tiniest piece of glass in the sole of her foot. Once it was dug out (insert drama), her foot felt fine. The pain had caused a limp, and under further observation, we discovered the source of the pain.

Sometimes we get so used to limping through life that we forget there's anything different. Pain is a known companion, one we believe will always be there. But it doesn't have to be. Probing for the source of our pain allows us to stop and deal with it. If the basis of our pain is sin, then confession is the first step to healing.

When we come to God and admit our mistakes with humility, we give Him permission to remove those sins from our hearts for good. This process might cause a little drama as bottled-up emotions rush out, and that's okay. Emotions are signals. They are also pathways to releasing all we've been holding inside. God made us this way. It's not easy to stop and confess. It's also not easy to accept God's complete forgiveness. We're people of habit, and changing our thoughts and actions is hard, even when our hearts have been changed.

In my daughter's case, we found it humorous that she still limped at times. Limping had become a habit. Sometimes, we do the same. Even though our heart is clean, our mind still remembers, and our responses have become routine. Our hearts are fully forgiven, but sometimes our minds disagree. I mean, how can such big sins be wiped out with one simple prayer?

As I learned through a Bible study for post-abortive women,[4] when we ask Jesus for forgiveness, He forgives all our sins, not just some. To choose sins that are "too big" for Jesus to forgive is the same as telling Him that His sacrifice wasn't enough. Telling ourselves we need to carry those "too big" sins by ourselves is a false narrative. We tell ourselves we shouldn't walk in freedom. We hand out consequences instead. The consequences we give ourselves, even after we accept Jesus's forgiveness, aren't just wrong—they're damaging. We still see ourselves as sinful in our own eyes and in God's. We struggle to draw close to Him because we feel we don't measure up, when the truth is, Jesus has already cleansed us and made us whole. Romans 3:23–24 says, "For everyone has sinned; we all fall short of God's glorious standard. Yet God, in his grace, freely makes us right in his sight. He did this through Christ Jesus when he freed us from the penalty for our sins." When we truly accept that our heart is transformed completely, we will feel less pressure to "do things right" or "make up" for what we've done. We allow ourselves to accept God's love, right here and now.

Your Turn

Take a few minutes to allow God to search your heart (Psalm 139:23). Is there anything you need to confess? Confess it. And after your prayer of confession, understand those sins no longer exist.

In their book *The Perfect You*, authors Andrew Farley and Tim Chalas write:

> Sure Jesus paid the price, but that price was not the cost of designing a specialized filter for God to look through. It was the cost of fundamentally transforming who you are at your very root. It was the cost of making you genuinely forgiven, genuinely righteous, and genuinely—not "positionally" but completely and truly—good.[5]

When we understand this, happiness fills our hearts. Without confession of sins, there is no room for God's love to dwell. But after we confess, a vast space opens up, allowing God's love to rush in.

Take time to rejoice in the newness of your heart. Do you feel God's love? Yes, it's been waiting for you all along. He's been waiting for you. Breathe in, breathe out, and in this moment, center your heart on this fact: *Jesus loves me, this I know . . .*

5 Minutes to Connect

1. Ask God to search your heart.
2. Confess your sins and mistakes to Him.
3. Imagine God wiping away those sins as if they never existed.
4. Embrace the knowledge that you are genuinely forgiven. Pray and ask God to help you see yourself that way.
5. Write down Isaiah 1:18 on a notecard and post it where you can see it: "Come now, let's settle this, says the LORD. Though your sins are like scarlet, I will make them as white as snow. Though they are red like crimson, I will make them as white as wool."

CHAPTER TWO

Life's Chaos, God's Embrace
The Secret of Surrender

I wait quietly before God, for my victory comes from him.

Psalm 62:1

Chaos came into the Goyer house in the form of children—many children. From 2010 to 2016, John and I adopted seven kids. First one. Then two. Then four. (We decided to stop adopting before we heard about a sibling group of eight!) Seven additional kids meant many needs and much mess. Yet the needs and the mess paled in comparison to the challenges of secondary trauma.

If you're unfamiliar with this term, "secondary trauma" is exposure to someone else's trauma. In our case, our adopted kids brought past trauma directly into our home. The kids came with duffle bags of clothes and garbage bags of toys. Some of them also arrived with attitude problems, attachment issues, and anger. Their hearts were jam-packed with resentment, fear, rage, grief, and loss.

All kids act out at times, but for many years, the battles were daily. As the mother figure, I often became the target. Seething, biting words from the mouths of teens pierced my heart. My own anger grew within, and along with it came both sorrow and shame. My life wasn't supposed to be like this. *I* wasn't supposed to be like this. Many days I questioned whether all the work was worth it. Was the care and love I offered making any difference? I'd flip between being assertive, attempting to gain control over the bedlam, and retreating, escaping from the tumult of tantrums and defiant disobedience. I found solace in my bed, where I'd pull the covers over my head, vacillating between crying, praying, and listening to audio Scripture to calm my frayed nerves.

This isn't how life was supposed to turn out. What's going to happen to us? How can I care for these children and all their needs? How am I going to survive this life?

This life.

This life wasn't the life I'd lived for the first two decades of marriage and parenting. Control slipped through my fingers like grains of sand. The impact of my children's past trauma—and their repeated, compulsive, and adverse actions—wore me down to the point of wanting to wave the white flag of surrender. Dealing with every small thing, over and over again, was just too much. My children's past trauma brought fresh trauma into my life.

Signs of secondary trauma include feeling numb or detached, feeling overwhelmed and hopeless. In the height of the conflict of the last few years, I became a shell of the thriving person I'd been before. Even before the pandemic toppled us, my heart hit rock bottom. Sinking into the abyss, I became angry at God for opening our hearts to adoption. I knew He cared for orphans and widows, but did He care for me? After all, our desire to follow God had led us to bring more pain into our home than I could have imagined— more than I could cope with.

Even though I was used to helping others and giving advice, my mind shut down amid my disillusionment. I couldn't respond to an email, let alone write a book. I had no energy and spent most afternoons (after struggling through a homeschool day) lying in bed. Sometimes I'd sleep. Other times I'd pray. This went on for months. Thankfully, my husband and oldest son filled in to help with the younger kids, but I knew things needed to change. My tight chest and racing heart clued me in that things couldn't stay as they were. My soul was depleted. Work piled up.

Achievement has always been "the great coverup" for me. To accomplish something and to receive praise helps to hide hearts that ache and ask, "Isn't there more to life than this?"

Maybe you also struggle with hiding your troubled heart behind achievement. Or perhaps you've learned to use humor as a "coping mechanism" to hide what's really going on. Some of my friends have admitted to using social media to create a facade that covers up depression and anxiety, hoping that if they reflect an image that all is well in their lives, they'll start feeling that way, too.

When people ask, "How are you today?" They expect us to answer, "Fine, and you?" although fine might be far from the truth. But we can only "fake happy" for so long. Even as Christians, we should not expect to be happy all the time. Yet, we would all do well if we took time to seek happy contentment from its true source: God.

We can fake happiness, but our mind knows the truth. Our heart, soul, and body do too. My body paid the price. I joked that my children's PTSD (post-traumatic stress disorder) gave me PTSD, but it was no joke. I started to have physical symptoms that accompanied the emotional trauma I faced, such as a racing heart, tight chest, and extreme fatigue. I got on blood pressure medication and a low-dose antidepressant. I started seeing a counselor, but deep down, I knew I needed to care for myself better than even that.

When the pandemic turned our world upside down and I had more time, I carved out moments for things I enjoyed (not just the things I did out of duty): I started watercolor painting. I baked and cooked more. I also returned to reading Christian fiction regularly—something I love but had put on the back shelf because big families take a lot of time to manage.

Yet, even more than self-care, I needed soul care. I needed to get back to the place where I daily spent time "getting my heart happy in the Lord." More than anything, I needed to rediscover the happiness of thirty-two years prior when I first prayed, "Here's my life, God. It's Yours." Even when I (again) had no idea where the future was leading, I needed to put my life completely back into God's hands.

Through the years, I'd taken back my life as my own. Without the heavy burden of my sins, I felt a new freedom to write, to serve my family, and to positively impact my community. I had true joy inside me, and I wanted others to feel the same.

Helping to launch a crisis pregnancy center helped me to see that my story could make a difference and that my hard work could help others. Then, when I started getting book contracts, readers let me know that the messages I shared mattered. The only problem was that volunteer and mentor, writer and speaker, became my identity. I showed up again and again because I couldn't imagine not showing up. Even when I felt near exhaustion due to the added kids and the added trauma, I continued to show up. Deep down my heart cried, "This is who I am, and this is what I do." I believed that if I dared to take a step back, I'd disappoint everyone, including myself.

Have you ever felt that way? Maybe you found purpose in a ministry that helped others. Perhaps one of your skills or talents grew into something people noticed and appreciated. Or perhaps part of your life has felt out of control, so you've compensated by finding ways to control other situations.

The problem is that when we become more focused on the doing and the fixing rather than being focused on God, it leads to a racing heart instead of a happy heart. And the truth is, no matter how much we work toward control, we will never be able to control everything. We also turn our eyes away from God as we attempt to manage all the good things we've gotten ourselves into.

Instead, true happiness is found in surrender. Peace and contentment come from lifting our eyes to Jesus, understanding that even if we don't get one thing done in the day, *we* are enough. More than that, a deep and intimate relationship with Jesus is enough.

For many years, I tried to save the world instead of simply depending on my Savior. Sure, I still read my Bible and prayed, but I'd figured out how to care for my own needs pretty well...until I got to the place where I couldn't. When I once again found myself in a dark place with little hope, Jesus brought His light. He showed me, step by step, how to turn (return!) to Him. My soul found rest in Him alone, and everything changed. As I spent time with Jesus, He reminded me that seeking more control isn't what I wanted after all. *He* was what I wanted.

I don't want to picture where I'd be if I hadn't worked on tending my soul over time. Just as growing plants can't be nourished by last week's sun, rain, and nutrients, neither can we. Every moment I spent reading my Bible, praying, and taking faith steps with God prepared me for the hard seasons that hit. Deep roots have helped me weather the storms. But even with deep roots, we all need daily tending. The daily tending reminded me that I didn't need to tackle everything myself. In fact, trying to do so gave me a racing heart that robbed me of my joy and peace. Each day, we need to find *heart happy* by choosing God's embrace, even in the midst of life's chaos. Striving for control in these chaotic times isn't the answer—turning to Jesus is.

Going Deeper

Heart Connection

When I was having significant behavior issues with our two-and-a-half-year-old adopted son (whom I'll call "Buddy," though that's not his real name), I took him to a children's behavior therapist to get help. I expected her to give me a list of ways to more effectively discipline him or ideas for calming his out-of-control nature. Instead, she assigned me the task of daily connecting with my son.

Since most of my day was spent telling him, "Stop" or "Don't do that," the therapist knew we'd both benefit from positive interactions. Looking back now, I also can see that she wanted us to make heart connections. After all, I had become the mom to an out-of-control child with whom I'd not bonded, and he'd become the son to an over-controlling mom he didn't know or care about.

My task was simple. The therapist wanted me to spend five minutes a day one-on-one with Buddy. This time had to be away from everyone else, giving him my full attention. My job was to create a box of special toys to enjoy together during these moments, and I was to follow his lead in what we played with.

I created a special toy box filled with simple games, plastic animals, and cars. As we played, my job was to:

- State what he was doing. ("You are lining up the cars.")
- Echo his words. ("The car is red.")
- Praise him. ("Great job sharing with Mommy.")

These interactions let Buddy know that I was focused and paying attention. It built a connection between us. A bond developed, too, which meant I didn't simply see him as a "problem child," and he didn't merely see me as "a woman who's always trying to stop his fun." As I began to enjoy these times with Buddy, I started treating him with more tenderness, and he started listening and responding. Buddy felt he was seen, heard, and appreciated. Amazingly, his behavior improved!

Looking back, I did this task with the goal of having my child listen to me and do what I asked. I wanted obedience, but as time went on, a bond was built between my son and me. There's no doubt that the therapist knew I wasn't bonded, just as Buddy wasn't. We needed a heart connection.

Your Turn

Too often, we sit down with the Bible with the same goal—we want a quick fix. We want a resolution to a problem. Either that, or we know we'll feel guilty if we don't spend time reading our Bible. After all, isn't that what "good" Christians do?

What we really need is to be bonded with God. We need His love. We need to open our eyes to what He is doing. We need to see God being active in our lives in good ways. We need to praise Him, too.

Before we praise, it's essential to pause to consider God's goodness, love, and care for us. This pause might just be the most powerful moment of our day. It's a redirection, getting our minds off the hard things in our lives and placing our gaze on the amazing Lord of the Universe, feeling His immense love for us.

---

5 Minutes to Connect

---

1. Say what God is doing—in Scripture, in the world, and in your life.
2. Repeat what He says. What are the words of Scripture speaking to your heart?
3. Praise His actions. Glorify God for who He is and all He's done.

Example

Scripture:

LORD, my heart is not proud; my eyes are not haughty. I don't concern myself with matters too great or too awesome for me to grasp. Instead, I have calmed and quieted myself, like a weaned child who no longer cries for its mother's milk. Yes, like a weaned child is my soul within me. (Psalm 131:1–2)

Say what God is doing:
In this moment and in my life, God is listening and present. He sees that I'm tending to my heart. He is present in my life by providing for me, connecting me with wonderful people, and helping me love and provide for my family in numerous ways.

Repeat what He says:

God is saying to me now that I don't need to concern myself with matters too great or too marvelous to understand. I can quiet myself. My soul can be still with His help.

Praise His actions:

I praise You, Lord, for meeting me here. I feel Your love in my heart. I praise You that you care for my soul. I praise You that I don't need to "fake" happiness with You. I praise You because, at this moment, I can feel the transformation happening in my heart, bringing stillness, peace, happiness, and joy. Thank You, Lord. Amen.

Connecting with God is as simple as that. Yet when we do it, everything changes. Our lives change, and our hearts change. Happiness floods in where it hadn't been before. Choose a scripture and try it, too.

CHAPTER THREE

The Priority of a Happy Heart
Receiving God's Love

*I have been crucified with Christ and I no longer live, but
Christ lives in me.*
*The life I now live in the body, I live by faith in the Son of
God, who loved me and gave himself for me.*

Galatians 2:20 NIV

If you've ever questioned why the Christian church is making so
little impact in our world, it's because, at the deepest level, our
souls feel exhausted. It's time to do something about this, starting
with ourselves. We need to care for our souls and bring our hearts
to a place of being "happy and satisfied." Only then will our lives
change, and only then can we do our part to bring positive changes
to the world around us. To do this, we need to make soul care a
priority in our lives now.

Each of us can find twice as many things to do than we actually have time for. How we spend our time is an indication of
what's most important to us. As the years have gone by, my priorities have changed as my heart has changed. Because I spend time
in God's Word, what's important to Jesus's heart becomes important to mine.

A few months ago, when I got up early to read my Bible, connect with God, and pray, one of my teen daughters was awake. She
hadn't been able to sleep and was lying on the couch. (I have my
"Jesus time" in the living room.) Soon, her twin sister joined her,
also unable to sleep. One teen lying on the couch quietly as I read
my Bible and pray is one thing, but two teens whispering and
goofing off wasn't working for me.

I set down my Bible with a sigh. "This is my time. I need it," I
said. "If you aren't Jesus, I don't want to hear from you right now."
(Yes, I really said that, and then I really did send those two girls
back to their room.)

That may seem harsh, but I've learned that spending time with
Jesus and cultivating a heart happy in the Lord is essential. I also
want my children to see that I take this time seriously, so I'm setting
a good example.

I need to find my "happy heart" before the day starts in earnest.
If I don't, my whole family suffers, and I do too. If I rush into my
day without spending time with Jesus, worries, fears, and frustrations are quick to overwhelm. If I don't take time to fix my thoughts
on God, my mind jumps from disturbances to distresses, and soon
it becomes too much.

A happy heart comes from feeling loved and knowing God is
present with me and in control. It also involves allowing His messages, found in the Bible, to turn my attention to what's really
important in the scheme of things. When I don't connect with God
to settle my heart, I feel as if it's me against the world. Everything
and everyone making demands of me, including my children,
become hindrances and obstacles to the life I think I deserve.

Yet when I take even five to ten minutes to read Scripture and
seek the heart-affirming messages that God has for me, everything

changes. I change from within. I don't need to fight for what I think I deserve because I understand that I'm truly loved and cherished by the God of the universe, and He will take good care of me. As His love flows in, it builds up a reservoir within me that then overflows toward others; my mind shifts from seeing them as obstacles to seeing them as people in need of God's love. Then I open my heart to opportunities to pour into others what God poured into me.

As I give my heart and time to connect with God in the morning—and throughout the day—I understand I don't have to live limited by my strength, stamina, or smarts. When I pause my body, still my heart, and focus my mind, my best life is possible as I access the power of Christ within me. As Galatians 2:20 reminds us, "I have been crucified with Christ and I no longer live, but Christ lives in me. The life I now live in the body, I live by faith in the Son of God, who loved me and gave himself for me" (NIV).

Jesus died so He could live a new life within us. We forget this. We fail to access the life of faith we can experience from God-in-us.

"The power that now animates, motivates, and propels your spiritual life is not you, but Christ! By grace, he makes you the place where he dwells," writes pastor and author Paul David Tripp in his devotional *New Morning Mercies*. "This means you are never in a situation, location, or relationship by yourself. He is always with you. And because he is always with you, you are never left to the limited resources of your own wisdom, strength, and righteousness."[1]

How do we go from fumbling through our day, feeling down and depleted, to truly understanding that Jesus is within us to influence, inspire, and initiate a new and different type of life? One of my favorite verses of all time is Ephesians 3:20: "Now all glory to God, who is able, through his mighty power at work within us, to accomplish infinitely more than we might ask or think."

We all want that, don't we—to allow God's mighty power within us to accomplish more than we ask or think? Where do we get this power? We discover the answer by looking one verse prior: "May you experience the love of Christ, though it is too great to understand fully. Then you will be made complete with all the fullness of life and power that comes from God" (verse 19).

The answer is as simple as A + B = C.

A: experience the love of Christ

+

B: be made complete with all the fullness of life and power that comes from God

=

C: [Jesus's] mighty power within us to accomplish infinitely more than we might ask or think

Life will never be perfect, conflict-free, or without hassles. (Don't we wish!) But peace to face the day with fullness of life and power blossoms out of experiencing the love of Christ. It's one thing to believe God loves us. It's another to feel His love from the center of our hearts.

The best way I know to experience someone's love is to spend time with that person. I enjoy date nights with my husband, John. I especially enjoy getting away together, but I can't depend only on weekly connections or more extended, focused weekends away to carry our love through.

As busy as we are with six other people living in the house (and an equal number passing through), our marriage would suffer if we didn't connect daily. I usually get up first and have my quiet time with God. Then, after John wakes up, we spend time reading the Bible and praying together. We also chat about our upcoming day and talk through any plans we need to make. We snuggle, and I send John off to work with a kiss as he makes the long journey to his office upstairs in our house. We also text during the day about various things. We sit near each other at dinner and hang out in the evenings. Then, at bedtime, we head to bed at the same time where our more personal time of intimacy and connection continues.

Experiencing each other's love throughout the day, even in the middle of an ultra-busy life, keeps our marriage strong. And you'd better believe there are a lot of interruptions. Numerous times a day, we have to tell the people in the house, "Wait your turn," when they try to interrupt.

When our children were younger, John and I made them sit at our feet and wait as we read the Bible together and prayed. There have even been times we've sent a child to his or her room for a few minutes so we could connect in peace—just as I did with my daughters who were being disrespectful toward me and my time with God.

I have to make time with John a priority, and I have to do the same with my time with God. I have to fight for this soul-tending time—at the beginning of each day and throughout the day—because I need it. If I'm going to live, I want to thrive. If I have to face the mountains of rush-more and do-more, I want to be surefooted. Otherwise, my days consist of feeling weary, alone in my battle, and unseen in my struggle. Why waste a day, a month, or a life living like that?

Of course, I don't want to give the impression that these priorities work perfectly every day. There are some days I don't wake up early because of long nights due to sick kids or work deadlines, and

I turn off my alarm instead of waking up. There are also times when I'm so consumed with something on my to-do list that I rush through my Bible reading and prayer or skip it completely. There also have been exhausting seasons, such as overwhelming kids' issues or health problems, when John hit snooze more often than not and we didn't have time to sit and connect. There were even seasons when the scary news of the world grabbed our attention, and John and I found our minds becoming more focused on what was "out there" than on what God wanted to do "in here," in our home and hearts. The good news is that each day is a new opportunity to refocus on what really matters.

Every Priority and Goal Is Set by YOU

Let me state this up front: No one in your life is as concerned about how well your soul is tended as you are (or should be). If you don't set soul care as a priority, no one else will. I promise you that.

As well as my husband loves me (and he does!), he's never gotten out his calendar and created pockets of time for me to nourish my soul. Yes, he's thankful when I've had my time with Jesus (mostly because my attitude is 100 times better), but he's never created that priority for me. Unlike our twelve-passenger van, no gauge tells my husband, or anyone else, that I'm empty and need my fill. My attitude declares that. (Watch out!) As handy as he is, John isn't going to be able to find a quick fix for my heart in those moments. Fostering a heart happy in the Lord is truly up to me.

My heart's happiness is not only up to me; it's the key to a thriving life. Yet there are seasons when I dismiss its importance. When things are going well, I forget how vital it is to draw near to

God. And then I suffer. I wonder why my soul feels empty, and even the good things don't hold the enjoyment they should.

That's because happy hearts aren't dependent on what one has or does. It's the inner workings that change the outward attitudes. If we were to compare suicidal millionaires with joyful grannies living on fixed incomes, it would become clear that what we believe about our lives, our things, and our worth is what matters.

We can look at our lives through lenses of gratitude for all we have or through lenses of dissatisfaction, feeling that we need more. We can look in the mirror and be in awe of who we are and what God has done, or we can see "not enough." We can believe we are someone designed by God, redeemed by God, and loved by God, or we can feel our lives have no meaning or purpose.

Happy hearts can be cultivated during unexpected life challenges, loss, and even pandemics. Sad to say, it's often during the times of hardship and heartbreak that I do a better job of paying attention to my soul and seek to make my heart happy in the Lord. Internally, I've been dead and dry during seasons that should have been full of abundance. I've also thrived during the heartbreaking and wearying seasons because I haven't been able to make it without the strength, peace, and love of God.

Nourished souls come from faithful tending. Knowing the need is the first step. Making it a priority to connect with God is the second. From there, God takes over. He meets us as we quiet ourselves to communicate with Him. The goal is not just to give us a dose of happiness to carry us through the day. The goal is to provide us with Himself and fill us with His love. Jesus is the light of this world, the Bread of Life, and our Living Water. When we invite Him into our hearts each day, they become happy because He is there. We need to prioritize connecting with Him and draw from

His unending well of resources. He's available continuously, but often we are not.

One of the problems with setting priorities is we don't know what we want. We have an elusive idea of the type of person we'd like to be, but we never turn this puzzling and romantic dream into a priority. When we understand the purpose of a happy heart and the goal of our soul, we can figure out the proper steps to achieve it.

The Goal of the Soul

Let's start with the basics. Human beings are made up of three parts: body, soul, and spirit, as discussed in 1 Thessalonians 5:23: "Now may the God of peace make you holy in every way, and may your whole spirit and soul and body be kept blameless until our Lord Jesus Christ comes again."

The body is prominent. It's our physical being. It's the part we shower and dress, move, and make still. Most of the world focuses on this outer part without understanding that our bodies are a small part of our complete makeup.

Our spirit is the eternal part of us—the breath of God within that gives us life and an essence that is different from that of every other created being. Genesis 2:7 says, "Then the LORD God formed the man from the dust of the ground. He breathed the breath of life into the man's nostrils, and the man became a living person."

Our spirit is the part of us that connects with God. It's our innermost portion that bridges the chasm to the supernatural realm. This bridge is not some mystical, invisible Golden Gate that floats between our hearts and Heaven. Instead, it's the part of ourselves that allows us to connect with the Living God—God's Spirit descends from Heaven to touch our spirit deep inside, uniting with us and validating our true selves. Romans 8:15–16 says, "So you have not received a spirit that makes you fearful slaves. Instead, you received God's Spirit when he adopted you as his own children. Now we call him, 'Abba, Father.' For his Spirit joins with our spirit to affirm that we are God's children."

Finally, our soul perceives things in the psychological realm. In fact, in Greek, the original language of the New Testament, the word for "soul" is *psyche* (which is also the root word of psychology). Our soul is our personality; it's who we are. With our soul (which includes our mind, will, and emotions), we think, reason, consider, remember, and wonder. We experience feelings of happiness, love, sorrow, anger, relief, and compassion. And we're able to resolve, choose, and make decisions.[2]

Authentic connection with Jesus involves all three parts—body, spirit, and soul. We physically control our actions and honor God by what we do. Our spirit joins with God to validate who we are. It's also the way we worship Him (John 4:24). Our soul, which includes our personality, emotions, and values, also needs to be surrendered to God. As we give God access to these areas which are encased in our mind, we break away from what holds us back and learn to live the abundant life God desires.

For example, 1 John 4:18 says, "Where God's love is, there is no fear, because God's perfect love drives out fear" (NCV). As we invite God's love into our souls, the more our fears diminish. Another verse that reflects the role of the soul—and its interaction with God—is Psalm 42:11: "Why, my soul, are you downcast? Why so disturbed within me? Put your hope in God, for I will yet praise him, my Savior and my God" (NIV).

As these verses (and many others!) show, when we surrender our souls to Him, God gently and tenderly removes the beliefs and emotions that are not beneficial to our lives as His children and replaces them with His truth.

Complete union with God comes as we still our bodies and give God's Spirit access to ours. Through this spiritual connection, God then has direct access to our souls, inviting His transforming work into every part of our being.

So many Christian lives lack transformation and vitality because we forget this last step. We may open our spirit to God on Sundays, but we don't pause long enough the rest of the week to renew this spiritual connection. More than that, we claim our souls as our own and cling to our individual nature with a vengeance. We claim our personalities as "the real me" and dismiss any flaws, weaknesses, and shortcomings as "just who I am." Either that, or we try to change, attempting to remake ourselves with our efforts—which never works—and then mentally beat ourselves up when we fail.

The good news is that as we connect with God's love and give Him access to our souls, change comes according to His wisdom and through His power. Our hearts are not something that need to be beaten into submission by our iron will or flailing fists. Instead, we offer our souls to God to mold and to fill. Fashioned after Christ and overflowing with God's love, a happy heart then becomes the staging ground where God is given access to every aspect of our personality, emotions, and values—and it's these things that guide our lives.

Remember what George Müller wrote?

> I began therefore to meditate on the New Testament from the beginning, early in the morning. The first thing I did, after having asked in a few words the Lord's blessing upon his precious Word, was, to begin to meditate on the Word of God, searching as it were into every verse, to get

blessing out of it; not for the sake of the public ministry of the Word, not for the sake of preaching on what I had meditated upon, but for the sake of obtaining food for my own soul.[3]

Müller continues,

The result of this is, that there is always a good deal of confession, thanksgiving, supplication, or intercession mingled with my meditation, and then my inner man almost invariably is even sensibly nourished and strengthened, and that by breakfast time, with rare exceptions, I am in a peaceful if not happy state of heart.[4]

Through his spirit, Müller opened himself to God. Once there, his soul guided him to confess his sins and flaws and to thank God. This also led him into supplication (prayers and pleading) and intercession (standing on God's promises for yourself and others). The spiritual connection is the beginning of soul reconstruction, leading to a happy state of heart and a different attitude toward life.

We have become powerless as Christians because we think the main thing is to give our lives to God once, asking Him to save us. Then we think it's up to us from there. Yes, submitting our lives to Christ is what gives us a new heart and access to eternity, but "giving ourselves to the Lord" should not stop there.

Our heart is happy as we surrender our complete selves to Jesus day by day and then live life (in our thoughts, emotions, and personalities) with Him throughout the day.

Think of it this way: our bodies move us through our moments, our spirits connect us with the divine nature of Christ, and our souls interact with God throughout the day, allowing Him to be with us, guide us, and transform us. What is the goal of the soul? To humble us and give Jesus the access and ability to do a makeover in every part of us.

Jesus's Soul Mission

Isaiah 61:1 is a prophecy that points to what the Messiah's mission on Earth is all about:

> The Spirit of the Sovereign LORD is upon me, for the LORD has anointed me to bring good news to the poor. He has sent me to comfort the brokenhearted and to proclaim that captives will be released and prisoners will be freed.

This is also the mission that Jesus lived day by day as He walked on Earth. Jesus even declared His mission by reading this prophecy in the synagogue (Luke 4:18). And it's the same mission He wants to achieve daily in your life and mine.

Happiness comes when the poor receive good news, when the brokenhearted are tended to, and when the captives and those in prison are set free. I've had the honor of interviewing both Holocaust survivors and the veterans who liberated them. There has never been a more joyous celebration than that of those locked in darkness and pain who see the prison gates open and their liberators enter.

What is Jesus's mission within you today? Could it be the same? Yes! Jesus's mission today is to anoint you with His presence. To preach the Good News to your mind. To bind up your broken heart. To proclaim freedom from your captivity of rush-more, do-more, and all the other unrealistic ideals that the world places on you. To release you from the prison of unworthiness that you find yourself in, to grasp the fact that you are worthy in Him.

The more I study about the soul, the more I understand we thrive when we involve all three parts of ourselves. In Luke 10:27, Jesus says, "Love the Lord your God with all your heart and with all your soul and with all your strength and with all your mind" and, "Love your neighbor as yourself" (NIV).

Truly loving God is an all-or-nothing thing. This is true union. Author Brennan Manning adds, "The deepest desire of our hearts is for union with God. God created us for union with himself: This is the original purpose of our lives."[5] As we pay attention, we can see that the men and women who had the closest relationships with God understood this unity. Here is an example concerning King David, whom God declared to be "a man after my own heart" (1 Samuel 13:14 NKJV).

In Psalm 16:8–9, David speaks of interacting with God in all three aspects of his being. He writes, "I have set the Lord continually before me; because He is at my right hand, I will not be shaken. Therefore my heart is glad, and my glory rejoices; my flesh also will dwell securely" (NASB).

Can you see the three different parts David describes? First, He prioritizes the Lord, declaring dependence on Him. Then his heart becomes glad, and his soul rejoices. With this happy heart, David is confident that his body will be taken care of, too.

These steps that David took thousands of years ago are ones we can take today. First, we can set the Lord before us and direct our thoughts toward Him. How we think about Jesus changes everything. Proverbs 4:23 says, "Be careful how you think; your life is shaped by your thoughts" (GNT). I've heard it said that we must practice turning our minds to Jesus. It's easier than that. As we commune with Him and make our hearts happy in the Lord, we fill up our souls with Him. As we give Him space in our thoughts, emotions, and self, His life outflows from ours.

John Eldredge writes in his book *Wild at Heart*,

> We come to believe deep in our hearts that needing anyone for anything is a sort of weakness, a handicap...Jesus knew nothing of that. The man who never flinched to take on hypocrites and get in their face, the One who drove "a hundred men wi' a bundle o' cords swung free," the Master of the wind and sea, lived in a desperate dependence on his Father. "I assure you, the Son can do nothing by himself. He does only what he sees the Father doing"; "I live by the power of the living Father who lives in me does his work through me." This isn't a source of embarrassment to Christ; quite the opposite. He brags about his relationship with his Father. He's happy to tell anyone who will listen, "The Father and I are one" (John 5:19, 6:57; 14:10, 10:30 NLT).[6]

It's okay to be needy—to turn to God to do within us what we cannot do ourselves. When I try to "practice" turning my mind to the Lord and living right, I always fail. Yet when I invite Jesus in, my soul is nurtured as this innermost part of me is filled with Him. When I make time to experience God's love, it becomes easier to dwell in it throughout the day. Soul care happens not because I'm practicing all the right things, but because Jesus within me changes things—and changes me.

Every part of us must be cared for—soul included. Soul care is different than self-care. Self-care often means nothing more than pampering. Self-care requires time to tend to our bodies and rest, but most of us don't have any extra time.

Soul care is for all people. All of us are weak. All of us grow weary as we tend to our daily tasks, serve the needs of others, and navigate the conflicts in this world—physically, emotionally, and mentally. As we care for our souls by allowing Jesus to care for us, we bring our hearts to a place of "happy and satisfied." Only then does change come. Yes, it's time to make this a priority.

Going Deeper

Making Time to Experience God's Love

If you don't set soul care as a priority, no one else will do it for you. Setting up a basic routine, guarding your time, and helping your family know your needs is the first step. I love these quotes:

> "Make margin for what matters. This is your one precious, crazy life. White space in your calendar is priceless. Why work so hard to fill it up? Aren't the in-between moments where we find the most joy?" —*Emily Ley*

> "The battle for our hearts is fought on the pages of our calendars." —*Bob Goff*

In the coming chapters, I'll share more insights about what I've learned about soul care. I'll share tools I've used and structures and systems I've set up. I'll teach you how to create fostering environments in your life and how you can teach others to tend their soul-nourishment fires. All of these are lovely things, but we're going to start small.

Below is a list of different ways to connect with God and experience His love. Read over the list. Which are the most meaningful (and doable!) for you?

Next, look at your calendar. What windows do you have in the upcoming week when you can take a few minutes to connect with God? Make a note of those times. Pencil them in. Developing this habit will take intentionality and time—but the more you see the growth and refashioning that comes, the easier it will be, and you'll even come to look forward to it!

Heart and Soul Connections

- Sit quietly and listen to worship music, reflecting on the lyrics and God's presence.
- Thank God for ten things from the previous day.
- Ask God to fill you with His love.
- Before you read your Bible, ask God to prepare your heart for His message.
- Read a passage of Scripture and ask, "Lord, please show me the blessing that you have for me within these words."
- Pause for a quiet moment, reflecting on who God is.
- Turn on your favorite worship playlist as you get ready for the day.
- Listen to a chapter of the Bible on an app, not to learn, but to listen to God's heart.
- Write out a Scripture that you'd like to memorize, and read it three to four times throughout the day.

- As you wake up in the morning, surrender your emotions to God.
- Ask the Holy Spirit to connect with your spirit in new ways.
- Share what you read in the Bible with a family member or friend.
- Pray with palms open, asking God to take the burden you're carrying that day.
- Choose one of God's attributes and praise Him for His character.
- Read a hopeful verse and add your name to it.

Your Turn

Did some of these soul connection ideas stand out to you? Suggestions from others are wonderful, but it's also important to dig deeper and contemplate our own thoughts. Here are some questions to get you started:

- I can make my heart happy in the Lord by:
- I desire the "goal of my soul" to be:
- I can prepare my body (physical state) to connect with God by:
- I can prepare my spirit (the eternal part of myself that connects with the Living God) by:
- I can prepare my soul (personality, mind, will, and emotions) by:
- I can set the Lord before me by:
- I can direct my thoughts toward God by:

Take time to think about what will work for you. Also, remember to come back to these questions during each new season of your life. Our circumstances change, and we change. We can always refine our ways to connect with God better for each season.

---

5 Minutes to Connect

God knows your heart and the season you're in. I asked some of my friends about their baby steps in starting a quiet time routine. I love these ideas! Consider taking five minutes to try some of them.

- "I used to say John 3:16 aloud to myself as I got out of bed each morning. The goal was to be consistent every morning and not pressure myself to do more. This gave God and me a point of connection during the overwhelming baby and toddler days." —*Jodi*
- "I start with a simple routine, making it a morning priority. I wake up, drink a glass of water, pour my coffee, sit down with a devotional (that includes Scripture passages), and journal. As I read, I focus on direction for the day. I pray, 'God, speak to me about Your plans and direction for the day.'" —*Michelle*
- "I have coffee already programmed to brew in the morning. Before my feet hit the floor, as I'm turning off my alarm, I thank God for the day and ask for His help. Then I get my coffee and Bible and sit down with a Bible study." —*Jenny*
- "One of the things that has helped me was to quit treating quiet time like an obligation, like cleaning my

kitchen or paying my bills. Quiet time is hanging out with Jesus, just like I like to meet up with a friend. It doesn't have to look a certain way. I put away the markers, journal, and big study Bible. Now I find videos on YouTube where someone is reading the Bible to me while I close my eyes and listen. Or I go for a walk and sit on a bench that looks out on something beautiful, and I talk to God. It doesn't have to look a certain way or happen at the same time every day. It only has to be the thing you most look forward to." —*Sharon*

- "I leave my Bible open where I can see it and read it as I get a moment. I also listen to praise and worship music on the way home from dropping the kids at school." —*Patricia*
- "I read the Bible—sometimes using the One Year Bible. I am blessed to have a teaching pastor who does verse-by-verse exposition from the pulpit, and that provides my in-depth study. During the week I attend a women's study and I read. Sometimes I copy Scripture. The act of writing cues a new part of my brain." —*Stephanie*

CHAPTER FOUR

The Sensitivity of God, the Sovereignty of God
Surrender and Trust

The eyes of the LORD search the whole earth in order to strengthen those whose hearts are fully committed to him.

2 Chronicles 16:9

Looking back, I'm thankful for every moment I sat before God with my Bible. I cannot remember the items on my to-do list from ten to twenty years ago, but I do remember the Scripture I memorized during morning walks. I understand complex passages of the Bible because I diligently study them morning after morning. I can sit, pray, and feel a soul connection with God today because doing so is familiar. It's as natural as making myself a cup of tea at the break of dawn and settling into my favorite comfy spot. As I still my body and force my soul (personality, emotions, values, essence) to relax, I have faith God will show up when I slow down, and I'm never disappointed. Daily diligence fostered a soul that can stand up against the cares of the world today and in days to come. And if you've only recently met Jesus, or have returned again to your faith, you can make the time now to build the habit of sitting before Jesus and reading the Bible as part of your soul care. Today is a perfect day to start!

As I've sat before God, this head knowledge has moved from my mind deep into my heart. I know with everything in me that God is sensitive, just as He is sovereign. Yes, God is an Almighty Ruler who holds the world in His hands and can change world events with the slightest whisper of His breath. Yet at the same time, His gaze searches the earth, seeking to find those who are committed to Him, as we read in 2 Chronicles 16:9. He wants to strengthen us, guide us, help us.

The problem comes when we forget this. We fail to remember that we do not have to face our struggles alone. More than that, even in the middle of a crisis, we tend to put others' needs before ours. Our minds may be reeling and our hearts breaking, yet we still worry about others and consider their wants and needs without realizing the pain is squeezing all life and hope out of our very souls.

For many years, I worked as the volunteer director of a crisis pregnancy center I founded. I learned during that time that women do a horrible job of caring for themselves, their needs, and their hearts. During a crisis, women often worry about what others think, pushing their thoughts and feelings to the side. When women then come to the heartbreaking point of considering an abortion, the person they think of last is themselves:

1. They think of their boyfriend.
2. They fear their parents' reactions.
3. They think about the baby.
4. Last, they consider themselves.

Concern about others' reactions outweighs what abortion will do to their bodies, souls, minds, and spirits. Many choose abortion because they believe it's what someone else wants, but these women are the ones who live with the consequences. They mourn the child their hearts have instinctively connected with, even in dire straits. Unable to deal with the pain, heartache, and shame of their hard choice, afterward many women attempt to block their emotions with drinking, drugs, promiscuity, or anything else that will numb them from regret and the reality of what they've done.

That was me. When I found myself pregnant for the first time at age fifteen, I worried about my boyfriend breaking up with me. I thought about my grandma's disappointment. I didn't want to face the embarrassment of having a baby, but I never considered how I'd handle the loss.

After the abortion, the knowledge of what I'd done crushed my soul. I erected a massive wall around my heart that stood tall and unyielding for many, many years. I also sabotaged myself by remaining in an unhealthy, abusive relationship, going to parties and drinking, and pushing away Christian friends, mentors, and even God. Thankfully, those Christian friends and mentors supported me when I became pregnant a second time and then chose to have my baby and dropped out of school. At my lowest of lows, they pointed me back to God. In my darkest place, feeling unloved and unworthy, I discovered God had been there all along.

This example is a biggie, yet to this day, I find I ignore my own needs as I tend to everyone else's. Maybe you're the same. We're quick to consider what others think and how our decisions will impact them. Yet rarely do we pause to consider what we believe or desire. During hardships, I attempt to be a loving spouse, caring mother, and helpful family member. I observe my neighbors' needs and find a way to help them. I attempt to encourage and inspire people online—not just hundreds, but thousands. Though mentally and emotionally spent, I work hard to live up to writing and speaking obligations because I know not doing so puts others in a difficult spot.

In an attempt to be a buffer between those I know and love and the hard stuff in life, I forget that the hard stuff is slamming against my mind, heart, soul, and spirit. But I can only stand up against the blows so long before crumbling. There's a fine line between being knocked down and being knocked out.

In our lives recently, a teen's struggles—and the ripple effect of heartache that it caused our family—made us forget there was a worldwide pandemic going on. One day I'd hold up my battered shield, trying to protect myself from the assault of words and actions, and the next, I'd dare to look up to find someplace to retreat for the tiniest bit of solace. The spiritual attack that came through her was so close and personal, I didn't have the time or emotional capacity to look beyond the walls of our home to the billions of masked faces around the world or the fear that filled their eyes.

When the blustering squalls of hardship refused to still during 2020, I was forced to care for myself in order to care for others. Even though I was used to getting a lot done in the day, during the pandemic (when I was tending to the needs and emotions of eight other people in the house without a break), I permitted myself to do less. Wearily, I'd tell myself, "You've done enough. It's time to rest." With Rush-more out of the way, I took Do-more off the plan, too. I ignored piles of schoolbooks, art supplies, work projects, and cleaning tasks for days and weeks. I gave myself permission to paint, bake, and cook instead of doing more productive things.

It wasn't easy, but I knew it was necessary. Sometimes we have to be honest with ourselves that we're going downhill fast. It also helps to step back and consider what advice you'd have for a friend. I'd probably say something like, "You're taking on a lot: work, special-needs kids, and your grandma, which would be hard enough in the best of circumstances. But lately, things haven't been the best of circumstances—not for anyone. You're struck by the disappointments and changes in your family, too. Give yourself grace. You can only do what you can do. Every day, consider what you need most: a nap, extra time reading the Bible (for soul nourishment, not out of obligation), hot tea and a good book, a chat with a friend, a nice meal, a bath. When you care for yourself today, you'll be able to better care for others. The same is true for tomorrow, too. Self-care isn't one and done. It's daily because the hardships of the world are daily, too."

Also, it's essential not to fall into the trap of thinking that we don't have to take time for self-care because we have it better than most. I've felt that way. I saw other moms thrust into a complete lifestyle change, having to work at home while teaching their kids. I believed I had it easier because I'd chosen the work-from-home and homeschooling lifestyle. I was ahead of the game. Over the years, I'd discovered how to manage both well.

Yet, pandemic schooling and working were different even for work-from-home parents and homeschoolers. Work didn't go on as usual because everyone I worked with was going through huge transitions. My kids' homeschooling activities were halted. And instead of spending the afternoons playing with friends in our neighborhood, we told them they could only play with each other during quarantine. We expected it would be a hard few weeks as everyone buckled down, but then quarantine stretched into months, and soon all of us greatly missed face-to-face connections with friends. I'm someone who loves staying home, but it became too much even for me.

While it helped to have compassion for others in this new situation, I had to give myself grace. I was going through a lot of changes, too. It wouldn't help my family or me if I refused to care for myself because others had it worse. Our needs are worth meeting—and we need to provide for ourselves just as we'd provide for others.

For many months, the house was messier, and my productive work slowed. I gave my soul breathing room. I permitted myself to be human and to understand that it's okay to consider my own needs. Can you relate? Do you often find yourself remembering to take care of others but forgetting to take care of yourself? Do you struggle to give yourself grace, even through hard changes? Do you somehow feel that your needs are not worthy of time and attention because others have it worse?

The best way to truly understand my vulnerabilities is to see myself through Jesus's eyes. More than anyone, Jesus was aware and sensitive to the needs of those around Him. Ever faithful, He cared for people well. Jesus's ultimate goal for His time on Earth was to become a living sacrifice to save our souls. Yet Jesus did not simply set His eyes on His ultimate goal. He saw the needs of others. He loved, cared for, and connected on a personal level.

There often is a massive difference between how we see ourselves and the way God sees us. I see "not enough." God sees "forever Mine, beautiful, chosen." God sees us as His children. He desires to love us, help us, heal us, and guide us.

We find one beautiful image of God's desire to guide His children in Psalm 37:23–24, which says:

The LORD directs the steps of the godly. He delights in every detail of their lives. Though they stumble, they will never fall, for the LORD holds them by the hand.

When we fall, God grips us tightly and raises us again. David, who wrote the psalm, experienced this.

Then David confessed to Nathan, "I have sinned against the Lord." Nathan replied, "Yes, but the LORD has forgiven you, and you won't die for this sin." (2 Samuel 12:13)

That's a compassionate God, isn't it? A God Who reaches out to raise us when we fall, even when falling, is a result of our own sin or mistakes.

Another beautiful verse that speaks of God's "hand-holding" is Isaiah 42:6, which says,

"I am the LORD, I have called You in righteousness. I will also hold You by the hand and watch over You, and I will appoint You as a covenant to the people, as a light to the nations." (NASB)

God holding your hand is not only a symbol of protection but connection.

Recently, I was speaking at a homeschool conference, and I took two of my daughters (ages eleven and thirteen) along with me. One evening, instead of going back to my room to rest, I took them to the waterslides at the hotel. While my thirteen-year-old went off to ride some of the bigger waterslides with our friend, my youngest wanted to play in the wave pool. As she splashed, I watched. Every minute or so, she'd look over to make sure that I was still delighting in watching her play, and she'd wave. I'd smile and wave back.

Since we're a family with many people in our house, my watching her was a wonderful time of one-on-one connection. And later, as we walked back to our room, dripping with every step, she reached out and took my hand.

"Mom, it's been a while since I've held your hand," she said.

I nodded and smiled. "Yes, but I like it."

She squeezed mine tighter. "Yes, me too."

Our time of connection at the pool drew my daughter to me, literally her hand to mine. She felt seen and loved. And when we spend time with God and lift our hearts to Him, we feel the same connection. We better understand His sensitivity and sovereignty. Just as I chose to be present with my daughter, God decides the same with us.

Trusting That God Cares

Some people believe humility is making ourselves less to combat pride. This is a false interpretation. In *The Perfect You*, Farley and Chalas write, "Real humility is simply seeing yourself as God sees you—no more and *no less*."[1] And how does God see us? Just look at how Jesus interacted with others daily. He brought the proud low, yet He lifted the shamed. He was encouraging, warm, and sympathetic. He not only wanted to heal people, but God also wanted to give them Himself. How Jesus cared for others is a perfect example of how we can help care for others and how we can better care for ourselves.

Every day, each of us cares for our current self and our future self. How would your day change if you managed yourself with encouragement, warmth, and sympathy? How would everything change if you didn't focus on your shortcomings, but instead took your brokenness and failures to Jesus and said, "Here You go. Do with me as you will."

We are fragile, but God fills us with His light. We are weak, but God has given us power. It is easy for us to be overwhelmed, but thankfully we don't have to face life—filled with heartache and troubles—alone.

A sensitive God inspired these words in 2 Corinthians 4:6–8:

> For God, who said, "Let there be light in the darkness," has made this light shine in our hearts so we could know the glory of God that is seen in the face of Jesus Christ. We now have this light shining in our hearts, but we ourselves are like fragile clay jars containing this great treasure. This makes it clear that our great power is from God, not from ourselves. We are pressed on every side by troubles, but we are not crushed. We are perplexed, but not driven to despair.

Knowing God cares for us, helps us, and seeks to comfort us is one thing. Yet even more challenging (in my opinion) is the reality that God allowed the pain to happen in the first place. To be candid, there have been many days when much of my hurt came from knowing that God was sovereign and could have stopped the pain from coming.

Even before the pandemic, I struggled with the heartaches that God allowed to enter my life. My biggest struggle came when one of our adopted teens brought anger, disruption, and grief to every part of our family. For months, her motto may as well have been

"Insert chaos here." She'd pick on other kids, stir up conflict in peaceful moments, and disturb everything she touched. She lashed out often, and I became her primary target. And it wasn't just about big things. If I dared to ask her to pick up her socks from the floor, there'd be flaming words and huge dramatic scenes. I'd find myself tensing up whenever she entered the room, and it hurt me to see so many people I love fall victim to her words and actions. It also frustrated me that her angry emotions controlled her. My daughter can be a true joy—but when she's not, she's *really* not.

During this time, my confused mind reflected my hurting heart. John and I had opened our home to kids from the foster care system when we were nearly empty nesters. I never expected things would be easy, yet I failed to predict how very, very hard they'd be. *Why, God?*

God knew the pain to come, and He still allowed it to happen. John and I had followed His call to open our hearts to orphans, yet I found myself crying nearly every day, beaten down and discouraged. Why would God allow such hurt when we were seeking to please Him? How could He know one person would bring so much hurt and lead us to adopt this child? I believed God was good, or rather, He *could* be good. It just didn't always feel like He was.

In moments like these, it was easy to forget how much God had done for me. Or how many times I've disappointed Him or hurt Him, yet Jesus still went to the cross to carry all of it so I could be forgiven. He forgave me of everything when I surrendered to Him, no matter the pain or hurt I caused along the way. Do you sometimes forget that, too? It's easy to look at our lives and think, "No fair!" while also forgetting what Jesus did for us. It's easy to focus on the hard stuff, not remembering that good can come out of it in the end.

Even though I didn't fully understand how hard things would be for John and me when we chose adoption, God is sovereign. He knew the pain *I* would cause, and He still chose me—He still chose us. It took me time to remember this and to be thankful that God adopted me into His forever family, knowing all the times I messed up and hurt his heart.

Still, all of us are prone to this forgetfulness. In the midst of pain it's nearly impossible to focus on anything else. When my teen rebelled, rejecting my love and breaking my heart, it hurt to know that God had seen that coming and allowed it. He knew the hard stuff that would hammer its way into my soul. He opened our hearts to adoption with the complete understanding that we would also hurt much because we loved much. He placed these kids in our lives, knowing that everything we had to offer would be rejected—at least for a time.

So while the world's focus was on a global pandemic, the crushing of my heart was due to situations that had nothing to do with a virus. There were many days I wept, and when the pain grew too great, trying to fix the situation wasn't going to cut it. Instead, I had to retreat.

In troubles and pain, sometimes a shield just won't cut it. In those moments, we need a fortress. I learned this with the help of a counselor. He taught me that there's a time to fight to help others, and there's a time to find a safe place to retreat. This was a hard lesson—to know that being in the fight wasn't helping my daughter, because she was going to do what she wanted to do, no matter the pain it caused. And it wasn't helping me. John and I made the hard choice to reach out to a family member for help, asking her to allow our daughter to live with her to give the rest of the family a bit of peace and time to heal. Thankfully our family member agreed. For that season, it was the right decision.

I accepted that it is impossible to try to fix others who have no intention of making the right choice. I also called in backup support by turning to friends who were willing to listen and to pray. I allowed myself to grieve this relationship that I'd poured love and attention into, to no avail. I accepted that I didn't have all the answers, and for a time, it was alright not to seek them.

The year 2020 taught me that surrender doesn't always mean failure, especially when one surrenders to God. By choosing to surrender, understanding that none of my efforts were helping anyway, I learned that it was alright—even good—to care for myself. I discovered that taking time to reflect and heal is vital.

Two books helped me during this time: *It's Not Supposed to Be This Way* by Lysa TerKeurst and *When God Doesn't Make Sense* by James Dobson. After reading both, my soul settled on one word: trust. I had to trust God even when my life was in chaos, my mind was in confusion, and my heart was cuffed and cracked.

Paul David Tripp talks about this type of trust in his book *New Morning Mercies*:

> The commands, principles, and case studies of Scripture will take you only so far in your quest to figure out your life. There will be moments when you simply don't understand what is going on. You will face moments when what the God who has declared Himself to be good brings into your life that won't seem good. It may even seem bad, very bad.... Real, sturdy, lasting peace that doesn't rise and fall with circumstances isn't found in picking apart your life until you have understood all of the components. You will never understand it all because God, for your good and His glory, keeps some

of it shrouded in mystery. Peace is found in trust of the One who is in careful control of all of the things that tend to rob you of your peace. He knows, He understands, He is in control of what appears to be chaos . . .[2]

Is it possible to have a happy heart in the middle of pain and chaos? The answer is yes. Even on challenging days, I drew close to God and found a safe refuge where I could trust in His goodness. I'm not sure how I could have handled life if I hadn't daily found ways to escape with God and cultivate a happy heart.

Sometimes Pain Is Part of the Plan

When life after adoption didn't turn out as easy as I assumed it would, the crushing and pressing of pain squeezed my heart. By calling us to adopt, God was calling me to hurt. Was pain part of the plan?

During pain, what we humans want most is relief. I wanted a child who would conform and who would be thankful for all the love and care we provided for her. Instead, she threw all her efforts into getting what she wanted: mainly to be out of our house to do whatever *she* wanted. The more I tried to love her and treat her with tenderness, the more she fought.

I discovered being loved is a scary place for some people. To accept love, you have to let down your defenses. You have to be vulnerable. For hurting people, lashing out and running is much easier.

To say I was stressed is an understatement. My aching heart turned into physical chest pains and panic attacks. In therapy with my kids, I've learned about triggers and fight, flight, and freeze reactions. Now, for the first time, I experienced them. There were moments when everything within me just told me to get into my van and drive far, far away. How could stress, chest pain, and panic attacks be God's best for me?

If John and I hadn't opened our home to kids through adoption, we'd be empty nesters. I'd have all day to write. We'd be able to travel. I'd have more time with my older kids and grandkids—at least that's the story I was telling myself.

And so I have to ask, what story have you been telling yourself? My pain is rooted in the trauma that came after adoption, yet all of us face different trials. Maybe your pain is rooted in broken relationships, illness, or singleness. Maybe financial struggles have pulled you down into a dark pit and you question God's ability to provide. Perhaps a great loss has overwhelmed your heart—a loved one, a home, or a dream. In the middle of the pain, it's easier to doubt God and to question Him than to trust.

In my heartache I withdrew, believing that God had tricked me into trading in a life of comfort for a life of pain. Then reality hit.

Who am I to say that the other life would have been better or easier? Honestly, how could I ever know if that "other life" would have been comfortable? Maybe John and I have all we have because God is sustaining us and blessing us for opening our home to more kids. Maybe the "other life" you've dreamed of would have different challenges. As much as we try to craft a perfect life with our minds, this world is still full of loss and hardship, regrets and pain.

More than that, nothing John and I have is provided by ourselves alone. Yes, we work hard, but the very breath we have comes from God. God is behind everything. He's given us the knowledge, wisdom, health, and strength to do the work we do.

All we have is from God. We came into this world with nothing and will leave with the same. The comfortable life that we have been striving for—expecting, even—is a figment of our imaginations. When in your life have you found the golden ticket, gotten to pass all the troubles, hit the jackpot, and headed directly to GO? Never? Me neither. Yet, we live as if everything should be better than it is, and when it isn't, we blame God.

Leaning into God

Facing my current struggles has caused me to lean into God like never before. What I see as a hard life, my adopted kids see as a good one. Yes, things are challenging at times, but they have a family. Yes, some kids have serious struggles, but we're all here to love them, support them, and help the best we can.

My life isn't just about me. Comfort is not the end goal, no matter what the commercials tell us. It's easy to cling to the hope, joy, and peace that the Christian life offers, but we often forget passages like this:

> Then Jesus said to his disciples, "Whoever wants to be my disciple must deny themselves and take up their cross and follow me. For whoever wants to save their life will lose it, but whoever loses their life for me will find it." (Matthew 16:24–25 NIV)

Stress suffocates, worries weigh us down, troubles throw punches at our hearts, and we find ourselves crying out, "God, are You there? Can You see me? Do You care? Can You do anything for this pain?" I wonder what God thinks as we wallow in misery and tears. It might be something like, "You're complaining about this, but you have no idea about the ways I'm caring for you, blessing you, and protecting you...no idea at all." And, when you think about it, we hurt because we love.

"The easiest way to keep from being hurt is to stop caring and to quit trying," my friend and fellow author Israel Wayne wrote on social media recently. "But that also means you have to stop truly living, so I wouldn't advise it. Sometimes, life is just going to hurt."

Israel is a popular speaker, husband, and homeschooling father of eleven. While two of his daughters were facing extreme health struggles, he found out their house needed major repairs. Knowing all that Israel and his family were going through brought thankfulness to my heart. First, I knew that God was taking care of Israel's family, just as He was taking care of mine, even in hardship. Second, it helped to see that other families also faced pain and hurt yet still turned to God.

Finally, it's easy to overlook changes that need to be made until they become too big to overlook. As one who always tries to be capable and do things on my own, I got to the place where I sought the help we all needed. My teen daughter's disruptive actions pointed to her inner disruption stemming from the trauma in her past. As I sought to bring calm to everyday life, I went to counseling for the first time and was reminded, "The power to fix things is not in your hands."

We found help for our daughter, too—counselors to guide her to inner healing and train her in life skills. For a season, she got excellent help—and maybe she'll be able to turn back to what she's learned in the future. I was also forced to my knees, learning to pray with consistency and desperation as I never had before.

What I saw as a life "out of control," I now see as life being set right…or at least starting down the right path. But it took the pain for me to do something about the problems. If things had only been slightly uncomfortable, I sadly wouldn't have made an effort to seek the help my daughter needed. Or the help I needed. And this brought me to repentance—but not in the way you may think.

According to Easton's Bible Dictionary, the Greek word for "repentance" is *metanoia*. The root is *metanoeo*, meaning "to change one's mind and purpose as the result of knowledge." This verb, with the cognate noun *metanoia*, is used to indicate true repentance, a change of mind and purpose and life.

We often think of repentance as simply seeking forgiveness, but it is actually taking time to trade our idea for God's idea. We believe one thing to be going on, but when we open God's Word, we discover His view of things. And because of that, our minds and actions change. When my fear turns to faith, that's repentance. When my sorrow becomes lined with hope, that's repentance. When my self-focused prayer expands to include a desire for God's will and God's glory, that's repentance. When I discovered I need to make soul care a priority because God sees it as a priority, that's repentance. God's Word brings His truth to light. God's Spirit confirms it in my soul, and things change.

I'm thankful for my change of thinking, even during tough times. I'm grateful that I understand better that God is not only in control of everything, He is also sensitive to our needs. Jesus, God-in-the-Flesh, was sensitive to the needs, fears, and shortcomings of the people around Him. He provided, and He cared. He cared, and He provided. When we can grasp that God is both sovereign and sensitive, our trust and faith in Him grow.

Going Deeper

All our lives, we're taught that surrendering means failing. We stumble, and then we must get right back up and continue the race, bloody or not. We believe that when someone needs help, we do whatever it takes to help them. And if what we're doing isn't working, it's because we just haven't figured out the right thing to do yet. But we need to remember that before we care for others, we need to care for ourselves.

When we seek to understand God's sensitivity, we can grow in tenderness with ourselves and our own needs. When we seek to understand God's sovereignty, we also discover how to trust. We can believe God is good and that He cares, even when times are hard. We can allow ourselves to be grasped by His hand. We can reach out our hands in trust toward Him.

Giving Ourselves Permission to Surrender and Trust

What do you need to give yourself permission for? Answer these questions.

Today, I give myself permission to:

Today, I will stand up for my needs by:

Today, I will care for myself by:

Then, when you discover positive ways to care for your soul, find opportunities to repeat them. These days, getting out of bed and grabbing my Bible, journal, and a devotional book is a habit, but it's a habit I've developed over time. I'm learning new habits, too, such as asking for help. I'm discovering that it's okay for us to feel needy, because it's often then we reach out for the help that others—especially God—desire to give.

Your Turn

Want to build positive habits around soul care? In his book *Atomic Habits*, author James Clear encourages "habit stacking," which is adding a practice you wish to incorporate onto a habit you already have. For example, I'm adding the habit of writing down a meaningful Scripture to my Bible-reading habit. I started by buying a nice journal and keeping it with my Bible. Then, when I pick up my Bible, I pick up the journal, too. What types of habits can you start stacking? Make a list.

5 Minutes to Connect

Thanksgiving and gratitude are wonderful habits to "stack." As we thank God for who He is and for His involvement in our lives, we lift our eyes off our problems and onto Him—where they should be. As you're going through your day, find something to thank God for with each new action. As you do, consider His attributes. Here are some to start with:

All-knowing
Approachable
Compassionate
Consistent
Faithful
Graceful
Holy
Just
Kind

Loving
Protector
Provider
Patient
Righteous
Sovereign
Trustworthy
Understanding

What others can you think of? Write them down.

CHAPTER FIVE

Let's Talk about a Happy Heart
Defeating Shame

Happy are those who are like this;
happy are the people whose God is the LORD.

Psalm 144:15 NCV

Even while I was coming up with this book's title, several people told me they didn't connect with the word "happy." Happiness is Disneyland, fresh-baked brownies, and finding a forgotten twenty-dollar bill in your pocket. Or is it?

According to the Oxford English Dictionary, happy is "feeling or showing pleasure or contentment." Achieving happiness isn't one and done. It's a state to be obtained again and again. It is changeable. And we all know how fast things change. A flat tire can ruin a road trip. The stomach flu can drain all the happiness from a beach vacation.

Yet happiness is also a state we can achieve. It's simply feeling happy or content in the moment. It's not being excited or blissful or even having great joy. It's having a sense that "this is good." Still, is this something we should strive for as Christians? Aren't we supposed to suffer here on Earth, knowing our reward is in Heaven? Is it even okay to try to be heart happy?

Psalm 1:1–2 says, "Blessed is the one who does not walk in step with the wicked or stand in the way that sinners take or sit in the company of mockers, but whose delight is in the law of the LORD, and who meditates on his law day and night" (NIV).

This happiness (often translated as "blessed") doesn't entail just sitting around and hoping God will send a blessing down. It's choosing to take the proper steps toward God.

There are two Hebrew words translated as "blessed." One is the verb *barak* (Strong's #1288), meaning "to kneel, bless."[1] The other is the noun *esher* (Strong's #835), which means "happy"; it is the one used in this passage.[2] This noun is derived from the verb *ashar* (Strong's #833), which means "to be straight."[3] In biblical terms, being happy isn't about acquiring *things*—it's not materialism. According to *Barnes' Notes on the Bible*, the Hebrew word for blessedness/happiness, *esher*, is a plural noun, from the root meaning "to be straight" or "right."[4] This word is different than how our society uses it. It's not just a momentary, light feeling. To be truly happy is to get our hearts "straight" or "right."

The Hebrew people saw two types of paths: the straight path and the crooked path. The straight path is the shortest distance between two points and is easy to follow. The crooked path is longer and filled with peril and fatigue, and one can quickly become lost on it. The "straight ones" are those who walk the straight path and are, as we would say, "happy."[5] By seeking a happy heart, we are setting ourselves straight. How? Through our connection with God. The opposite is choosing to do our own thing. It's picking a path of our own design where we get fatigued and feel lost. There's nothing happy about that.

Tending our souls and focusing on being heart happy isn't something we'll figure out overnight. In a world of quick fixes, tending takes time. But instead of being discouraged, let's consider this good news. We can lower our expectations concerning suddenly "being fixed." Instead, we can make small shifts that tilt us in the right direction. One small change leads to another small change and then, months from now, we can look back and smile at the positive shift.

Is "Happy" Wrong?

If we were seeking happiness from the things in the world, this would be a wrong motive. Being happy isn't about getting something—it's not about materialism. In the book *Money, Possessions, and Eternity*, Randy Alcorn writes,

> Materialism results from a failure to realize that we were made for only one person (Jesus) and one place (heaven). Those of us who know Christ will one day be with him in heaven. Until then, nothing else can satisfy us. Materialism is a lie that Satan whispers in our ears: "If you had this thing or this person, you'd finally be happy." As long as we live by the lie, regardless of what we say we believe, we will be practicing materialists.[6]

True happiness is an emotion derived from God. Therefore, when we seek heart happiness, we must seek God. As humans, we understand when our heart is not happy.

"Every man, whatsoever his condition, desires to be happy," wrote Augustine. "There is no man who does not desire this, and each one desires it with such earnestness that he prefers it to all other things; whoever desires other things, desires them for this end alone."[7]

A person carrying the burdens of shame and regret does not have a happy heart or a contented soul. Confessing our sins and accepting God's forgiveness brings happiness. A new and clean heart then gives us the freedom to live the life of abundance and joy that God intends for us.

Charles Spurgeon wrote, "My dear brethren and sisters, if anybody in the world ought to be happy, we are the people. How large our obligations! How boundless our privileges! How brilliant our hopes!"[8] Yet, this isn't often taught to us as believers. Instead, we focus on joy and skip over the happy part of the Gospel. Knowing that, here are some things that are important to remember:

Happiness can be more than a me thing. It can also be a we thing.

Psalm 33:12 says, "Happy is the nation whose God is the LORD—the people he has chosen to be His own possession!" (CSB). As Christians, we not only should be individually happy but corporately happy. Could you imagine how attractive this would be to the world if it were true?

We will be heart happy when we follow God's ways and understand all the good things He desires for us.

In his book *Does God Want Us to Be Happy?*, Randy Alcorn asks:

> What if a happy God made us for happiness, and therefore our desire to be happy is inseparable from our longing for God? What if God wired his image-bearers for happiness before sin entered the

world? What if wanting happiness isn't the problem, but looking for happiness in sin is? What if our desire to be happy can be properly redirected to God and all that he wants for us?[9]

Alcorn is not speaking of the prosperity gospel. God has so much more for us than that. Exodus 19:5–6 says, "Now if you will carefully listen to me and keep my covenant, you will be my own possession out of all the peoples, although the whole earth is mine, but you will be my holy nation and serve me as priests" (CSB). What could be more exciting or bring more heart happiness than that?

Our happiness reflects our understanding of where we stand in Christ.

Happiness is not an emotional thing. It's a positional thing. We are children of God, and we have access to Him at any moment of any day. He is with us. Of course, this doesn't mean we always have to be smiling and bouncing around as if we're out of touch with reality.

We've done a lousy job of making happiness an emotional thing by connecting it with outward bravado. We've forgotten that none of the emotional hype is needed—none of it. We don't need outward enthusiasm and outlandish antics to get the attention of God. All He requires is for us to make a straightforward request: "Jesus, become Lord of my life."

I was honored to care for my grandfather during the last months of his life, when he was eighty-three. He lost his first wife and child while he was serving in World War II. After marrying again, Papa had three daughters and worked at a factory until he retired in his sixties; only after all that did he become a Christian.

He and my grandma lived in a mobile home, and they cared for their family well.

After giving his heart to Jesus, Papa gave up drinking and settled into a simple life of fishing, cutting wood for his stove, visiting family, and mowing his neighbors' lawns just to help out. I don't remember Papa ever standing in front of the church to speak, and when he sang the hymns and worship songs, I'd strain to hear his voice.

Yet I do remember him sitting down every morning with a cup of coffee and his Bible. I also remember him praying for each family member by name, "Dear Jesus, be with Tricia today. Keep her safe. Be with her at school. Help her on any schoolwork or tests she has today." Tears fill my eyes even now, remembering that.

Papa never went on a mission trip, and I'm not sure if he ever read the Bible all the way through. He loved cowboy movies, his small garden patch, his family, and Jesus. And that was enough. How do I know? Because on his last conscious day, Papa saw Jesus.

My grandma had been praying with him, and Papa started talking about the beautiful flowers he saw and their aromas. He spoke of the beautiful birds and the lion.

"Oh, if I were an artist, I'd paint that lion," he said. Then he lifted his hands and started praising Jesus. Papa told us he saw Jesus there, arms outstretched to him. Never a demonstrative person, the only time I ever saw my Papa with his arms raised and tears on his face was the day Jesus showed up to welcome him home.

Think about the sermons you've sat through. Well-meaning pastors and Bible teachers want us to do what is right. They explain the rules of the Bible. They warn us of judgment for doing wrong. They mix encouragement with threats. They provide "promises" of the good that will come when we obey, and they pile on the guilt when we don't.

As well-meaning as they are, as numerous as these messages are, we start to believe that our Christian walk is more about what we do than who we are (a sinner saved by grace and a child of God). When I start to feel that I'm not doing enough, I think of Papa. He gave his heart to Jesus and loved those closest to him. That's all that matters when you really come down to it. The elaborate way that Jesus welcomed Papa into Heaven reminds me of that.

God desires for us to change, but actual change comes from internal transformation, not external manipulation. Every commitment to "do things differently" lasts a few hours (or at most a few days). If we attempt to change by our own will, we will always fail.

Actual change—heart-happy change—comes from the inside out. The closer I grow to Jesus, the more I allow him to "do His good work" within me. I am different because of my love for Him and my willingness to let Him do a good work in my heart. Only this kind of change will last. A happy heart that's in the process of being transformed by Jesus changes our view of our circumstances, not the other way around.

Faith Is Not a Formula

Since I talked about Papa, I need to share about Grandma—who still lives with me—too. She is ninety-two and the perfect example of heart happiness. Her work each day consists of eating, napping, and watching black-and-white cowboy movies. Yet, she is genuinely heart happy.

Grandma is thankful for those who care for her. She praises God for "the day that the Lord has made." She communes with

God in song. I know because I hear her at 3:00 a.m., singing to Jesus. Grandma still has a sense of humor, too. When a nurse or therapist comes to visit, she always claims she's twenty-nine and pretends to be upset when they object. Grandma also loves to show off her "dancing," holding on to her walker and swaying her hips. She still has excellent sway after all these years. If Grandma based her happiness on what she could accomplish, she'd be the saddest person on earth. But she's not. She loves Jesus, and she knows that Jesus loves her.

There's a difference between knowing the rules of Christianity and personally connecting with Jesus. The Pharisees were a religious group of men who made following God's laws their life's work—but when God walked among them, they missed Him. I understand this.

One day, I was in the middle of my very ritualistic morning Bible reading when I felt God tap my heart. "You spend a lot of time learning about Me. Are you ready to connect with Me?" He said. The answer was yes.

I put aside my study guide and simply sat. I closed my eyes and leaned my head against the back of the couch. I pondered my journey with Jesus. I thought of the little girl who'd heard about His love in Sunday School and who whispered prayers to Him in her dark bedroom, feeling His love in return. I remembered being the teen who attempted to find love to fill the chasm within her heart and instead finding herself pregnant and abandoned. And then, when she surrendered, discovered Jesus loved her no matter the state she found herself in.

As I thought about all these things, my chest warmed, and a quiet peace fell over me like a soft blanket. Knowing that Jesus stood at His father's side yet also reached down to me at that moment caused fresh tears of joy to spring to my eyes. The worries of the day fell away from the forefront of my mind as my soul reminded me that Jesus created me for Himself, not for all the things I could do for Him.

That day started the same as a thousand other days, yet it shifted my outlook. It was similar to pulling back a curtain to allow in the sunshine. I'd been able to see just fine before, but pushing aside the "work" of spending time with Jesus allowed new light to flood in.

Like most followers, when I dedicated my life to Jesus, I separated things into two categories: *do* and *don't do*. It became easy to focus on the don't-dos and then beat myself up for not being a good enough Christian. As much as I willed myself to be joyful, kind, loving, and patient, I could never achieve that goal. And when I tried to stop being drawn to the wrong type of television shows or books, I wondered if I should be trying to tell others about God when I didn't have my act together. I mean, why should people listen to me when I claimed to be a Christian and still messed up again and again?

The more time I spent just being with Jesus, enjoying His presence and His love, the more I found myself no longer drawn to the media that the world offers. It became distasteful to me. Like how, after I learned to cook from scratch at home, those boxes of mac and cheese just didn't cut it anymore.

When we focus on a relationship with Jesus over religious rules, we experience God's presence in our lives in ways we didn't believe were possible. Faith is not a formula. We can believe in Jesus and live a pretty good life. Yet when we experience God, feel His love, and join Him in His work in the world around us, everything changes.

Yoked with Christ

We all know the formula of reading the Bible, praying, attending church, and telling others about God. Still, when we feel flat in our faith, we believe it's because of our failings. Without the heart-to-heart connection with God, we attempt to trust in the formula, but that gets us nowhere. Without a happy heart, we tend to believe we're not doing enough of the right things. Then we start to think our belief is lacking too.

- When troubles and worries come, we chastise ourselves. "I'm not giving it to God."
- When prayers go unanswered, we think, "I don't have enough faith," even though only a mustard seed's worth is required.
- When difficult circumstances come into our lives, we worry we're not claiming victory over our hardships or putting on our armor as we should.

Much of Christianity is pointing out ways we're not doing enough, but the whole point of Jesus coming is that we *can't* do enough.

One verse that has spoken to my heart in the last year is Matthew 11:28–30, which in the Amplified version reads:

Come to Me, all who are weary and heavily burdened [by religious rituals that provide no peace], and I will give you rest [refreshing your souls with salvation]. Take My yoke upon you and learn from Me [following Me as My disciple], for I am gentle and humble in heart, and you will find rest (renewal, blessed quiet) for your souls. For My yoke is easy [to bear] and My burden is light.

I cannot help but think of the book *Farmer Boy* whenever I read the word "yoke." Laura Ingalls Wilder's books were my favorite growing up, and I love sharing them with my children. Recently, I read *Farmer Boy* to my ten-year-old son at bedtime, and this passage reminded me of the gentleness of Christ as we take on his yoke of discipleship:

> Star and Bright were in their warm stall in the South Barn. Their little red sides were sleek and silky from all the curryings Almanzo had given them. They crowded against him when he went into the stall and licked at him with their wet, rough tongues. They thought he had brought them carrots. They did not know he was going to teach them how to behave like big oxen.
>
> Father showed him how to fit the yoke carefully to their soft necks. He must scrape its inside curves with a bit of broken glass, till the yoke fitted perfectly and the wood was silky-smooth. Then Almanzo let down the bars of the stall, and the wondering calves followed him into the dazzling, cold, snowy barnyard.
>
> Father held up one end of the yoke while Almanzo laid the other end on Bright's neck. Then Almanzo lifted up the bow under Bright's throat and pushed its ends through the holes made for them in the yoke. He slipped a wooden bow-pin through one end of the bow above the yoke, and it held the bow in place.

The passage goes on, and its gentleness touches my heart. Almanzo was gentle in his training, as his father had taught him. The purpose of the yoke was to teach the calves how to behave when they became big oxen.

Like Almanzo, Christ is gentle in His training of us. Jesus wants to remove the burdens of religious practice from us and show us a better way, leading and teaching us gently. Yet sometimes, it's hard to distinguish the difference. I've discovered that discipleship comes from conviction, whereas religious bondage comes from shame. I realized this anew from a recent sermon I heard.

Often, when I speak at different churches, I have an opportunity to visit one of the services. That day, the pastor's sermon was from the Old Testament, and he was comparing the hard-hearted Israelites with today's generation. He talked about how we've walked away from God's way, especially parents who are not training children as they should. He gave many examples, and with each one, I felt burdens of shame pressing down upon me. One was this:

"Parents today give time for other things, but they do not gather their children around them for devotions and Bible readings in the morning and at night, and then they wonder why their children go astray."

With each additional example, shame upon shame settled on my heart. I felt like a failure as a parent. My chest tightened, and my stomach became uneasy. In those moments, listening to those words, I was discouraged, not encouraged. I scolded myself for not doing enough to train my children and wondered why I thought I should be speaking and teaching at all. *Shame. Shame. Shame.*

I felt unsettled as we left the church. Even the next day, I felt guilty that I hadn't been as diligent as I should in my parenting.

Only after I sat down with my Bible the following day did I feel the burden lift as I read:

> These words I am commanding you today are to be upon your hearts. And you shall teach them diligently to your children and speak of them when you sit at home and when you walk along the road, when you lie down and when you get up. (Deuteronomy 6:7 BSB)

While this passage says we need to teach our children God's truth at home and away from home, when we go to bed and get up, nowhere in the Bible does it speak of twice-a-day devotional time. I'm sure that devotions—a Scripture passage illustrated by a thought or a story—are modern and not something believers have been doing for generations.

I also considered our family. John and I talk about God often during the day. We share personal stories of what God is teaching us. We answer our kids' questions. I teach my kids about the Bible and biblical truths during our homeschooling activities. We attend church as a family, and we often serve others together. And at least once a week, one of our teens asks a question about God and faith (usually around bedtime); those conversations go deep and typically take a while to sort out.

No, we do not have morning and evening devotions together as a family, but when I feel a stirring within me that I need to spend more time with a specific child, I do. With the Holy Spirit's leading, I feel impressed to take time to train or disciple. It's very different from the shame I felt from that pastor's chiding.

I love how the Amplified version expands on this Scripture (Deuteronomy 6:7):

You shall teach them diligently to your children [impressing God's precepts on their minds and penetrating their hearts with His truths] and shall speak of them when you sit in your house and when you walk on the road and when you lie down and when you get up.

Just as Almanzo knew to be gentle with Star and Bright, God is gentle with us as He teaches and leads us. And we are to be the same way with our children. "Impressing" and "penetrating" happens when something is soft and moldable, including young hearts. And even though many "parenting mandates" come from good intentions, religious rituals can quickly become burdens when we follow them out of shame.

Have you felt the same shame? We can feel guilty when we don't read our Bible in a day. We can feel ashamed if we have to miss church or we don't have time to volunteer as we think we should. Yet guilt and shame should never be motivators. Doing things with the wrong intentions doesn't draw us closer to the Lord; it does the opposite. We become weary, and these types of burdens are hard to shake. After all, even if we get it right one day, we often can't keep up our streak day after day.

Instead of attempting to live up to these standards, peace comes when we listen for the still, small voice of Jesus, who says, "Come, I have something to teach you. I want to lead you. Don't worry. I'll be gentle."

Jesus desires for us to have rest and renewal for our souls, which comes from connection with Him, not religious rituals. And then, as we learn from Jesus, we can do the same as we lead and guide our kids.

Give Your Burdens to Jesus

As you read the section above, did you feel your burdens lifting? Does this concept of depending on Jesus—not your own efforts—seem doable? Are you beginning to believe that faith has more to do with a relationship than a formula? I hope so. I hope these words make your heart happy and bring peace, joy, and rest.

Recently, we have faced unprecedented challenges on a global scale. All our lives have been disrupted, and each of us has desperately attempted to keep our tiny universes in order. It's been overwhelming and exhausting.

Yet, what if keeping our world in order (or attempting to) isn't the point? Instead, Acts 17:26–28 says:

> From one man he created all the nations throughout the whole earth. He decided beforehand when they should rise and fall, and he determined their boundaries. His purpose was for the nations to seek after God and perhaps feel their way toward him and find him—though he is not far from any one of us. For in him we live and move and exist. As some of your own poets have said, "We are his offspring."

As we read in these verses, what if our whole purpose is to "feel our way" toward God and find Him? According to *Ellicott's Commentary for English Readers*, the Greek word for "feel after" expresses the act of groping in the dark.[10] Think about that. In the history of the world, you were meant to live in this moment—in this darkness—for one purpose. The reason? That you would have significant needs and unmet longings, and in your searching for answers, somehow grope for God.

As Paul David Tripp writes in *New Morning Mercies*:

> Rest is never to be found trying to figure it all out, because you never will. There will always be mystery in your life. God will always surprise you with what he brings your way. You will always be confronted with the unplanned and unexpected. All of this is because you don't rule your own life and you don't write your own story. And the One who does rule and write doesn't tell you everything about your life and his plan. No, he tells you things you need to know to live as you were designed to live, and then he graces you with his presence and his power...Rest is only ever found in trusting the One who has everything figured out for your good and his glory.[11]

In our darkness, groping and questioning, we discover that God is not far from any of us. When we choose to yoke ourselves to Jesus, we find He is close. He is connected to us, directing the way and shouldering our burden. Sometimes the yoke appears to hold us back—but from what? Being lost, feeling alone, and choosing the wrong path. Is that the type of "freedom" we desire?

My third son, Nathan, was prone to wander as a toddler. From the time he could walk, he'd head off in any direction without a parting glance over his shoulder. He'd never look back to see if I'd follow. He wasn't concerned about me being around to keep him safe.

I told this to a friend once, and she didn't believe me. When I set Nathan on the ground, he took off. My friend tried to slyly follow him at first, hiding from tree to tree, but then she realized that hiding wasn't necessary. I was right. He never looked back. It wasn't until Nathan headed toward the edge of the murky pond that my friend scooped him up and brought him back to me. She and I knew the dangers that awaited if I didn't keep Nathan close. As much as he longed for freedom, I knew what was best. And the truth is, Jesus knows what's best for us, too.

> See, I have set before you today life and prosperity, and death and adversity; in that I command you today to love the LORD your God, to walk in His ways and to keep His commandments and His statutes and His judgments, that you may live and multiply, and that the LORD your God may bless you in the land where you are entering to possess it. (Deuteronomy 30:15–16 NASB 1995)

These verses continue: "So choose life in order that you may live, you and your descendants, by loving the LORD your God, by obeying His voice, and by holding fast to Him . . ." (30:19–20).

How wrong we have gotten the Christian life? How much time we have wasted thinking that following Jesus is all about knowing a set of rules and following them in our own strength! Living by a strict set of rules was never the ultimate design. It's time to root out the shame. It's time to stop learning about God and connect with Him instead. It's time to become heart happy, just as God designed us to be.

Going Deeper

Shame is a feeling of judgment. Shame starts by making us feel uneasy but then can grow into the torment of guilt.

In *The Power of Shame*, Agnes Heller writes:

The feeling of shame is the same effect which makes us conform to our cultural environment. The eye of others is the stimulus which triggers the feeling response and the expression of shame: it makes us blush, hide our face, it arouses the desire to run away, to sink into the earth, to disappear.[12]

I experienced those feelings when the pastor whose church I visited spoke against those who did not do devotions morning and night with their children. I looked down to my lap, and heat rose in my cheeks. I wanted to disappear. I felt unworthy, especially as someone who would soon be speaking to the women of that church. Yet shame is not from God. Instead, God speaks to us through His Word and with His Spirit through conscience and conviction.

When we have a clear conscience, we have peace. When we follow our God-given convictions, we feel happy or joyful. Both conscience and conviction are the gentle yokes that God uses to train and lead us. When we read God's Word and think, "I want to do things differently. Lord help me," that's a good thing. We seek God, asking Him to guide us. With Christ, we work toward change.

Earlier in this book, we discussed confession that stems from giving our whole lives to God. Yet beyond that, there will be many, many more times to confess. 1 John 1:9 says:

If we [freely] admit that we have sinned and confess our sins, He is faithful and just [true to His own nature and promises], and will forgive our sins and cleanse us continually from all unrighteousness [our wrongdoing, everything not in conformity with His will and purpose]. (AMP)

Is your heart full of love for God? Is your love for Christ the center of all you do? Do you long for Jesus in the middle of who you are?

I don't ask these things to bring guilt, but rather to point you to the one thing that will change everything: love for God from deep in your heart. If this center feels cold and dead, don't be discouraged. Each of us can turn to Him for help and say, "Lord, help me to love You more. Lord, move into the middle of me. I welcome You here. I want to welcome You here as I never have before."

Your Turn

Make a list of the things that have made you feel shame. One by one, take those things before God. Confess. Then ask Him to replace the shame with a right conscience and the right convictions from Him.

5 Minutes to Connect

Take a few minutes to write down the different paths you've taken in life. Thank God for how He has helped you to shift away from the bad paths with His grace and guidance. Also, praise Him for the good paths He has led you to. Then, sometime this week, find someone to share your story with. Pray and ask God to begin, even now, to soften the heart of someone who needs to know the heart happiness you've found in following God.

CHAPTER SIX

Scripture Nourishment, Prayer, and Listening to God's Voice
The Power of Prayer

The instructions of the LORD are perfect, reviving the soul.
The decrees of the LORD are trustworthy, making wise the
simple.

Psalm 19:7

God's Word, the Bible, is the source of nourishment for our souls. That's easy for me to say now because I've been a student of it for twenty years. I've taken Bible classes, but most of my knowledge has come from good books that have taught me about the Bible. Looking back, I knew very little about it as a young mom and new Christian. Sure, I had attended church for much of my life, but what I had picked up was more like a collection of stories than a comprehensive understanding.

I'll date myself by saying that I loved Bible story flannelgraphs—paper cutouts of Bible characters with flannel on the back that would stick to a cloth-covered board to make a kind of diorama. My Sunday school teacher would read a story from the Bible and put the characters onto the board for illustration. While I did know about Jesus feeding the five thousand and Daniel in the lions' den, I had no idea how all those different stories fit together.

When I tried to pick up the Bible as an adult, a lot of it didn't make sense. What do the exploits of Israelites and Hittites have to do with us now? What's up with angels with flaming swords and riders on horses? Is this science fiction?

Having a basic understanding of the type of literature found within the Bible is a good place for anyone to start (I recommend the book *What the Bible is All About* by Henrietta Mears for anyone interested in the subject). It's amazing how God's Word can speak to us and nourish our hearts, even with the little we know. We don't have to try to figure it all out. Instead, each day we can turn to God's Word and seek to understand one small truth.

Remember what George Müller wrote?

> I began therefore to meditate on the New Testament from the beginning, early in the morning. The first thing I did, after having asked in a few words the Lord's blessing upon his precious Word, was, to begin to meditate on the Word of God, searching as it were into every verse, to get blessing out of it; not for the sake of the public ministry of the Word, not for the sake of preaching on what I had meditated upon, but for the sake of obtaining food for my own soul.[1] ... The result of this is, that there is always a good deal of confession, thanksgiving, supplication, or intercession mingled with my meditation, and then my inner man almost invariably is even sensibly nourished and strengthened, and that by breakfast time, with rare exceptions, I am in a peaceful if not happy state of heart.[2]

Reading Müller's words from centuries ago makes me smile. Why? Because his routine then is the same one I follow now. It's as simple as 1, 2, 3, 4.

1. Ask God to open your understanding before you read.

James 1:5 says, "If you need wisdom, ask our generous God, and He will give it to you. He will not rebuke you for asking." The Bible is God's message to us, yet it's not easy to understand. It consists of sixty-six books, written by forty authors over 1,500 years. These books are written in various styles. There are books of history and poetry. Some chapters read like newspaper reports. Others read like fiction.

Yet, no matter the writing style, the Bible is the Word of God. It is helpful to find a resource that can help you better understand the various types of literature in the Bible. It's also good to remember that even if we don't understand everything about the passage we're reading, God can still use those words to speak to our hearts.

Ask God for wisdom before you read. Pray that He will guide you to the truths He has for you for that day. Pray that you will connect with Jesus as you read.

2. Choose a short passage.

Start in the New Testament if you are new to the Bible. Reading the Bible should be about discovering truth and building a connection with Jesus. I have followed reading plans, and they have been helpful and encouraging, but the goal of sitting down with the Bible should never be checking a box on a to-do list.

In general, the New Testament is written straightforwardly, and it's easier to understand than the Old Testament. The first four books—Matthew, Mark, Luke, and John—each share the story of Jesus, and they are easy to follow. Even reading one small section is a great start.

3. Meditate on God's Word.

Lately, the word "meditate" has gotten a bad rap. Mindful meditation, which is popular these days, involves conscious breathing to build attention and mindfulness. A person stills his or her body and mind to create space and focus; it brings awareness to oneself. While we all need focus and space, a better type of meditation is turning our mind and focus to God's Word. It's seeking to understand the Bible and God's plans and desires through the help of God's Holy Spirit.

Reading through the gospels—the first four books of the New Testament—it's clear that everything Jesus said was a complete change in the predominant thinking of His time. Even His closest disciples didn't understand the parables He told, and they asked Jesus repeatedly to explain them.

Even after His resurrection, Jesus explained everything they'd just seen and experienced, including His death and new life. Luke 24:44 says,

> Jesus said to them, "These are the words I spoke to you while I was still with you: Everything must be fulfilled that is written about Me in the Law of Moses, the Prophets, and the Psalms." Then He opened their minds to understand the Scriptures. (BSB)

What happened then can also occur with us as we take time to connect with Jesus and meditate on the Word of God. As we open the Bible and read, there will be things we don't understand. Biblical meditation is different from the popular form of meditation, as it does not consist of emptying our minds of all thoughts. Instead, it consists of focusing on the verses before us, pondering them, and asking Jesus to open our minds to understand them.

Meditating on Scripture moves Bible reading beyond a lovely habit. It gives God's Word a chance to take root in our hearts and grow. Joshua 1:8 says,

> This book of the law shall not depart from your mouth, but you shall meditate on it day and night, so that you may be careful to do according to all that is written in it; for then you will make your way prosperous, and then you will have success. (NASB 1995)

Of course, these concepts of prosperity and success have nothing to do with the world's definition of both. What the world considers prosperity—wealth, possessions, and the approval of man—is actually what keeps the truth from sinking into our hearts. Jesus speaks about this in the parable of the sower. There are many things to keep the seeds of God's Word from taking root. Mark 4:18–19 says,

> The seed that fell among the thorns represents others who hear God's word, but all too quickly the message is crowded out by the worries of this life, the lure of wealth, and the desire for other things, so no fruit is produced.

The New International Version translates "the lure of wealth" as "the deceitfulness of wealth." In Greek, the word "deceitfulness" can also mean "delusion." When we think of wealth, we think of comfort, ease, and peace; that is a delusion. We never get to a place of enough, and there is no peace in that.

Still, we allow everything "out there" to distract us from the message that God desires to speak to our hearts. We take time to read God's Word, yes, but it's soon forgotten as we race off to all the busy and vital things we've added to our day.

Biblical meditation allows us to pause and consider the message. It urges us to invite Jesus into our space and open our minds to the truths found in the Scriptures. Meditating on God's Word can lead to a peaceful, happy state of heart, no matter what is going on, knowing the God is aware and in control of every situation in our lives. We start considering our actions and interactions in light of the truths we've read. Of course, this doesn't happen overnight.

"Information can come immediately, but revelation is normally a process," writes Dutch Sheets in his book *Intercessory Prayer*:

> As the parable of the sower demonstrates, all biblical truth comes in seed form. Early in my walk with the Lord, I was frustrated because the wonderful truths I had heard from some outstanding teachers were not working for me. When I heard the teachings, they had seemed powerful to me. I left the meetings saying, "I will never be the same!" But a few months and weeks later, I was the same.
>
> As I complained to God and questioned the truth of what I had heard, the Lord spoke words to me that have radically changed my life: *Son, all truth comes to you in seed form.* It may be fruit in in-person sharing it, but it is seed to you. Whether or not it bears fruit depends on what you do with it. Spiritual information seeds must grow into fruit-producing revelation.[3]

4. Follow your soul's leading in interacting with the message of the passage.

As you read God's Word with contemplation and openness, your soul will start to respond. You might desire to confess, worship, or pray. You may consider a change in your life. Small insights and minor changes will transform everything.

Sometimes you may be led to take action or to move in a new direction. This has happened numerous times in my life. My decisions to help start a crisis pregnancy center, to mentor teen moms, and to adopt children came out of moments when I sat with God's Word, felt Jesus stirring a new direction within me, and then rose to respond.

Of course, this may seem like a scary concept to some. Perhaps you're afraid that God will call you to adopt a lot of kids or move to Africa. The good news is, the things God calls you to will flow from your gifts, talents, convictions, and mission. Usually, these calls don't come out of the blue. Instead, they are confirmations of ways He's already been working.

Also, Jesus will never ask you to do something and then leave you alone to try to get it done. (And I'm so glad!) Instead, we should see the Bible as the road map to guide us as we walk with Jesus. Instead of finding road signs pointing the way to go, we find a Savior standing there waiting. Can you imagine His smiles as He turns to you and says, "Alright now...here we go."

I love the way Henry Blackaby explains it in his book *Experiencing God*:

> Who is the one who really knows the way for you to go
> to fulfill God's purpose for your life? God is! Jesus said,
> "I am the way, the truth, and the life," (John 14:6).

He did not say, "I will show you the way."

He did not say, "I will give you a road map."

He did not say, "I will tell you which direction to head."

He said, "I am the way." Jesus knows the way; He is your way.

If you were to do everything that Jesus tells you one day at a time, you always would be right in the center of where God wants you to be.[4]

Isn't that a relief? When you get to the place where you trust Jesus to guide you one step at a time, you will experience new freedom. You can read God's Word with an open heart, knowing that if Jesus has a new direction for you, He will be leading you. Along every path, Jesus is there, and we see this as we turn to Him in prayer.

Turning to Jesus in Prayer

We often feel like weak prayer warriors when we sit down to pray and our minds wander. Instead, as we read God's Word, we can see prayer as a natural conversation with Jesus that flows out of what we are reading. We don't have to search for things to pray about. Instead, it becomes a natural outpouring. As we read, we may pray for a change within. We may pray for the needs of the world around us. We also may lift our voices in prayers of forgiveness and prayers of dedication.

The more our Bible reading leads to prayer, the more we see that Scripture isn't mere words on the page. Scripture is powerful and penetrating. As Hebrews 4:12 says, "For the word of God is alive and powerful. It is sharper than the sharpest two-edged sword, cutting between soul and spirit, between joint and marrow. It exposes our innermost thoughts and desires."

When we pray, we are giving Jesus a welcome invitation to work in the world and in our lives. We have weak prayers because we haven't experienced impossible prayers being answered. Desperate prayers should be an everyday occurrence, not just a last resort.

My first true desperate prayer was asking God to "do something with my life" as a teen mom. My second desperate prayer was praying for a future husband who loved God and who would love my son and me. God answered both in amazing ways.

After living thirty-one years as a Christian, I often find myself in situations where I will fall flat on my face unless God shows up—and I have seen Him show up again and again. Whenever I've faced chaotic circumstances and turned to Jesus, I've found Him there. Whenever I've dared to take steps of faith, I've turned to Jesus, and I've seen Him there. Whenever I've questioned a new direction, I've turned to Jesus and found Him there, too, walking with me step by step.

Opening Ourselves to Guidance

God's Word teaches us how Jesus is with us, guiding us and protecting us. As Psalm 23:1–4 says:

> The LORD is my shepherd;
> I shall not want.
> He makes me lie down in green pastures;
> He leads me beside quiet waters.
> He restores my soul;

He guides me in the paths of righteousness
for the sake of His name.
Even though I walk through the valley of the shadow of
death,
I will fear no evil,
for You are with me;
Your rod and Your staff, they comfort me. (Psalm 23:1–4
BSB)

The Living God, through His Word, does one or more of these things in the course of my mornings. When I sit down to connect with Him, He settles me and cares for me. He brings inner renewal. He guides me and wipes out my fears. He protects my heart and comforts me, and so much more.

Even as I typed out this Scripture, its truth penetrated my heart. The rod and staff—God's shepherd's crook—defends me. No matter what painful thing lies ahead in my day, God's Word helps me to trust that Jesus will provide His guidance and protection as I encounter it. The rod and staff are used to direct the sheep and even to bring minor chastisement. The rod is also used to protect the sheep from enemies, and knowing that God is strong against any attack on me brings me peace.

My mind and heart also focus on the words "the valley of the shadow of death." I took a virtual tour of Jerusalem yesterday, and the tour guide showed us "Heaven" and "Hell." Heaven was represented by the Temple Mount in Jerusalem—or Mount Moriah—and Hell was represented by the Hinnom Valley. The Hinnom Valley is an actual place where pagans worshipped the demonic god Moloch; as part of their worship, they would sacrifice their children in fire. When the Jews returned to Israel after the

Babylonian exile, this valley became a garbage dump, where fires continually burned to control the waste. *Hinnom* in Hebrew is translated as *Gehenna* in Greek; *Gehenna* is where we get the English transition "Hell."

On the tour, I learned that, in biblical times, when traveling to Jerusalem from the south, one had no choice but to pass through the Hinnom Valley. This is the route that Abraham and Isaac took when they were headed to Mount Moriah for Isaac's sacrifice. At the end of his path through the valley of the shadow of death, Isaac found life, and from his loins the nation of Israel was later born.

God's Word this morning connected with what I'd learned yesterday and provided hope for me today. No matter what I face, God will be there to guide and protect me. What started as an illustration for this book transformed my morning and made my heart happy as I felt God's guidance and sensed this was a message for me now.

As I read God's Word, I was reminded of God's care and protection, and I prayed for myself and for those I know, including one of my children. She is currently choosing to walk away from God's path—but doesn't God's Word also say that He leaves the ninety-nine to go after the one (Matthew 18:12–14)? Even as she wanders, the Lord's rod and staff will protect her. As I rise from my reading and prayer, there is a renewed peace and joy that wasn't there before. My happy heart trusts in God's care.

Stilling Ourselves to Listen

It's easy to understand that talking to God is one part of praying, but listening is equally important. As we meditate on His Word and listen to what it is speaking to our hearts, we gain new insights. We might consider a change in our thinking or our actions. We start to align our thoughts with God's. We might even feel God speaking to us—perhaps not in an audible voice, but with clear direction all the same. We gain confidence in our decisions because we know the One who is guiding us.

We often hear Christians say, "God told me," and we wonder how those believers were given the remarkable ability to hear from God because all we hear is silence. While God can speak in an audible voice, He usually speaks in other ways. In *Experiencing God*, Blackaby writes, "God speaks by the Holy Spirit through the Bible, prayer, circumstances, and the church to reveal Himself, His purposes, and His ways."[5] For me, I feel God "speaking" when I read a scripture and consider its application. Later, I might notice how that truth can be applied to my life in the middle of my day. Later yet, a friend might bring up the topic in a conversation, or I might hear a sermon or a podcast discussing the same thing. Even later, when I talk to a friend or a family member, he or she might confirm changes that need to happen. Not once did I hear an audible voice from Heaven, but the change of direction I felt was apparent—a message from God, given and confirmed in numerous ways.

Perhaps you've experienced this, too. Maybe you heard something in a sermon that really made you pause, and then a song on the radio brought that truth to your attention again. Even later there could have been a sunrise that stirred your heart or a new joy that filled you during your morning walk. Since we're all different, God speaks to us differently. Yet it's wonderful to know that as we continue to seek God, He will make His desires clear.

While setting up a routine and learning to turn our hearts to God can be as simple as "1, 2, 3, 4," we must remember there will be times when it feels like the words we're reading are flat. There will be other times when we pray that our prayers aren't answered as we wish they would be. It's essential not to give up. Dry seasons of the soul can come even in the midst of our seeking. It's also vital to remember that God's answers are correct, even when they aren't the ones we want.

Why Aren't Our Prayers Answered?

Sometimes we ask for what we need, but the answers don't come. Here are some reasons the Bible gives for that.

1. We pray with the wrong motives.

Sometimes our motive may be to make life easier for ourselves. For so many years, I prayed about my kids' problems because I was weary from dealing with their behaviors and wrong choices. God convicted me by asking, "Are you praying for them or yourself?"

To truly pray for someone is to allow God to soften your heart toward them. It desires God's greatest good for them, for their sake and not yours. Also, by praying for God to fix others, we ignore all the ways *we* need to change. Pointing out someone else's faults is easier than dealing with our own, isn't it? Pride keeps us from wanting to give our lives to God. Pride hijacks our prayers.

Jesus talks about this in Matthew 7:4–5:

> How can you think of saying to your friend, "Let me help you get rid of that speck in your eye," when you can't see past the log in your own eye? Hypocrite! First get rid of the log in your own eye; then you will see well enough to deal with the speck in your friend's eye.

For many years I prayed for my kids, "Lord, change them" when I should have been praying, "Lord, change me." Yes, my young adult kids need to make changes in their lives, but I haven't always handled my role as a mom well. I flip between wanting to micromanage their lives and throwing up my hands and declaring, "Fine, if you're making that choice, then you get to deal with the consequences!"

The truth is, God hasn't called me to make my older kids act right. If anyone could have "made" people do that, Jesus could have, but He didn't. God also doesn't want us to walk away, even though it seems easier to disengage than to have our hearts broken over and over again. In both cases, we're praying, yet we're also attempting to maintain control of the situation.

Other times, our motive is to get things we think we deserve but don't need. James 4:3 says, "When you ask, you do not receive, because you ask with wrong motives, that you may spend what you get on your pleasures" (NIV). God is not interested in giving us things that He knows won't be in our best interest.

2. *We pray for answers, but we're unwilling to give up control.*

In his book *Emotionally Healthy Spirituality*, Peter Scazzero writes:

> I like control. I like to know where God is going, exactly what he is doing, the exact route of how we are getting there, and exactly when we will arrive. I also like to remind God of his need to behave in ways that fit with my clear idea of him. For example, God is just, merciful, good, wise, loving. The problem then, is that God is beyond the grasp of every concept I have of him. He is utterly incomprehensible.[6]

Sometimes we pray and then stick to the path we've already decided is best for us. Sometimes we pray, and we don't want to give up seeking the pleasures of this world, even as we ask God to help us and to fix things.

Sometimes we pray for God to change us, but we don't take steps to be different or do things differently. Sometimes we pray for others, and when we don't see things happening quickly enough, we step in to try to fix them ourselves.

When I found myself pregnant at seventeen, no one stepped in and tried to fix my life. And I'm glad. First, I wouldn't have appreciated it. Second, no human person ever could have fixed me or my circumstances. The only One who was capable of doing that did. Jesus didn't just put band-aids on the mess I'd made; He gave me a new heart. It was what I needed. It was all I needed.

Also, even though I was a pregnant teen with a hard heart and a "leave me alone" attitude, my mother, grandmother, and other Christian women pressed in. They invited me to join their Bible study without being pushy. They visited me to pray without lecturing me. The pastor's wife (Darlyne, who is now my mother-in-law) sat in the room and quietly prayed, even when I wouldn't let her come close, even when I turned my back and pretended she wasn't there. Her simple presence reflected love to me and softened my heart to others. Her prayers softened my heart to God, too. Darlyne's prayers and time proved she was invested in my soul—not because she wanted her way, but because she desired God's best for me.

Matthew 6:33 says, "Seek the Kingdom of God above all else, and live righteously, and he will give you everything you need." When we seek God's best for ourselves and others, we know the answer will be according to what He knows we need. But over-coming prayers do take time and persistence.

3. We forget that prayer is a spiritual battle and persistence is needed.

2 Corinthians 10:3–4 says:

> For though we walk in the flesh [as mortal men], we are
> not carrying on our [spiritual] warfare according to the
> flesh and using the weapons of man. The weapons of our
> warfare are not physical [weapons of flesh and blood].
> Our weapons are divinely powerful for the destruction
> of fortresses. (AMP)

These phrases are military terms. Prayer is a weapon in the fight for good against evil. Prayer is us joining the battle against spiritual enemies that attack the soul. Persistence is needed to bring down fortresses in the spiritual realm, just as in the physical realm. When we pray, we must remember that our need to keep praying is part of the fight and that Jesus will bring victory in the end.

4. We get discouraged when we don't get an immediate answer.

How often did people in the Bible receive the answer they wanted during the time frame they wanted? Hardly ever. When God told Abram, "Leave your native country, your relatives, and your father's family, and go to the land that I will show you" (Genesis 12:1), He didn't hand him a GPS. Abram couldn't Google Maps the location beforehand in preparation. Instead, he had to start walking into the unknown. Hebrews 11:8 says, "It was by faith that Abraham obeyed when God called him to leave home and go to another land that God would give him as his inheritance. He went without knowing where he was going."

When we make plans for our lives, we think we know where we're going, but it's only an illusion. No matter how detailed the plans we make might be, we can't see the future or the obstacles to come.

The good news is that God sees what's ahead, and He knows what's best for us. Peace comes when I remind myself, "God loves me completely and is directing me on the very best paths for my life. I simply need to take the next step I feel He's leading me to."

Instead of trying to see the whole path ahead—which is impossible—surrendering ourselves to God's plans gives Him access to our hearts and minds. Then, with hearts open to His direction, we're content with doing the next right thing and taking the next God-directed step.

An old hymn from 1834 perfectly describes how this should be.

> The night is dark, and I am far from home,
> Lead Thou me on!
> Keep Thou my feet; I do not ask to see
> The distant scene; one step enough for me.[7]

For me, the phrase "one step enough" stirs something in my heart. It's true faith. True trust. As I pondered these words, I did more research on this hymn, *Lead, Kindly Light*. Written first as a poem by a young priest far from home and unable to travel, this hymn has strengthened men and women in challenging times.

Allegedly, in 1909, thirty English miners trapped underground in an accident that left 168 of their co-laborers dead sang it until they were rescued. Marion Wright included it during a hymn-singing gathering on the *RMS Titanic* and later on the ship's lifeboats as the steamer sank into the icy waters of the Atlantic Ocean.[8] And

Betsie and Corrie ten Boom sang these words with other women as S.S. guards led them to the Ravensbruck concentration camp during the Holocaust.[9] These are a few recorded instances, but how many times has a worried and wearied soul received the courage to face the unknown path before him or her by singing these words?

We have only two options when following God: trust or doubt. We can choose to rely on, believe in, and find assurance in God—or not. There is no middle ground. And even when the answer doesn't come immediately, we must continue strong in prayer with faith that God leads us rightly.

James 1:5–8 says,

> If you need wisdom, ask our generous God, and he will give it to you. He will not rebuke you for asking. But when you ask him, be sure that your faith is in God alone. Do not waver, for a person with divided loyalty is as unsettled as a wave of the sea that is blown and tossed by the wind. Such people should not expect to receive anything from the Lord. Their loyalty is divided between God and the world, and they are unstable in everything they do.

Doubt is allowing life's circumstances to toss you around. True faith stands firm in the storm. Our illusion of control can never be trusted, but God can.

Courage comes when I understand I never have to face the problems of this life alone. Contentment comes when I see myself as forgiven and when I know everything I have has been generously given to me by God. As Psalm 18:32–33 says, "God arms me with strength, and he makes my way perfect. He makes me as surefooted as a deer, enabling me to stand on mountain heights."

5. We often don't take the time to go to Jesus in prayer because we forget just how much He loves us.
In his book *Care of Souls*, David G. Benner writes,

> As presented in the Gospels, [Jesus's] primary method of soul care was dialogue. Jesus strove to lead people toward repentance and a conversion that would flow out of the heart and into every sphere of life. His was a message of salvation, of new and abundant life. He proclaimed this message through word and deed to all whom he encountered. While verbal instruction was certainly present, his frequently indirect and even paradoxical methods of teaching suggested that he not simply sought cognitive assent to his teaching but a total reorientation of life. Jesus's approach to soul care was based upon his conviction of the immense worth of persons.[10]

Those who spent the most time with Jesus understood that God deeply valued them. John called himself "the disciple whom Jesus loved" (John 21:7 NIV). He understood it, embraced it. The stories of imperfect people loved by a perfect God fill the pages of the Bible. That's good news for us.

Jesus did more than just give advice—He gave Himself. Change doesn't come by the outward things we do. Change comes as we present Jesus with complete access to our hearts through prayer.

God's Spirit within us desires to bring healing so that we may move toward wholeness. God's Spirit within us strives to sustain us so we may endure whatever comes in a day. God's Spirit within us reconciles, re-establishing our broken relationship with Him and others. God's Spirit within us offers to guide, helping us make the right choices, grow in wisdom, and mature into women (and men) of God. All of this starts with remembering how much we are loved and by continuing to pray.

Going Deeper

The Message version of Psalm 19:14 says, "These are the words in my mouth; These are what I chew on and pray. Accept them when I place them on the morning altar."

Meditation is a simple way of taking the truth of Scripture and thinking about it—or chewing on it. To be able to meditate, you need:

1. Quietness. Turn off the television, your music, your computer. Let your mind ponder your favorite scriptures and think of God.
2. Discipline. What are your values? What do you want to carry through your day? What does God want you to cut out so you can have more of Him? Discipline yourself to only allow into your life what's best for your day.
3. Structure. Creating a habit of meditation helps us to turn to God regularly. When we take time to ponder God's goodness, our meditation rises to Him in sweet prayers. God desires for us to fill our day with thoughts of Him. He wants to be our constant companion, and this happens when we take steps to allow room for His presence.

Your Turn

Read over these words from the hymn *Lead, Kindly Light.*

The night is dark, and I am far from home,
Lead Thou me on!
Keep Thou my feet; I do not ask to see
The distant scene; one step enough for me.

Now, answer these questions.

The dark in my life right now is:
I feel I'm wandering in:
I need God to guide me in:
The next step I feel God leading me to is:

The answers might not come all at once. Continue to bring them before God with persistence, seeking Him for peace, wisdom, direction, and faith to take the next step. Keep chewing on them until you discover God's message for you. Allow God to care for your soul even in the midst of your seeking.

5 Minutes to Connect

What is one of your favorite hymns? Look it up on the internet and read through the lyrics. Pause on the words or phrases that stir something within your heart. If you don't have a favorite hymn, read these lyrics from "Amazing Grace."[11]

Amazing grace, how sweet the sound
That saved a wretch like me
I once was lost, but now am found
Was blind but now I see
Twas grace that taught my heart to fear
And grace my fears relieved
How precious did that grace appear
The hour I first believed

CHAPTER SEVEN

Worthy, Not Abandoned
Understanding Your Value

So be strong and courageous!
Do not be afraid and do not panic before them.
For the LORD your God will personally go ahead of you.
He will neither fail you nor abandon you.

Deuteronomy 31:6

I mentioned something in the last chapter that I don't want to skim over. I wrote, "We often don't take the time to go to Jesus in prayer because we forget just how much He loves us." If we don't understand how much God loves us, we'll never get to a place of being heart happy. I believe much of this stems from a heart of abandonment. When we question if God is there or if He even cares, we're unwilling to open our hearts to Him. Can you relate?

In the last year, my soul care has involved looking back at my life and seeing the root of where my heart of abandonment started—then coming to peace with my past and understanding that although I've been hurt and felt abandoned by people, allowing God entrance into my soul brings healing. It also allows me to turn to God instead of holding back.

I was born to a single mom, and I lived with her and my grandparents during my early years. When I was eighteen months old, my mom moved many states away for a few months. She was gone—and that was painful for me as a child.

My mom married my stepdad when I was four years old. We lived in the same mobile park as my grandma, and I'd often sneak out to go to my grandmother's house. Even now, I can remember the warmth of her place. There was laughter, good food, and peace. The lack of expectations upon me nurtured me. The unconditional love made me strong. It felt like home.

Growing up, I knew my mom loved me—that was clear. Still, the environment at our house wasn't the same as at Grandma's. My mom and stepdad had my baby brother; he was theirs. Deep inside, I felt set apart. Even in the various rental houses we lived in through the years, my room was set apart.

My room was usually down the hall or in the attic, away from everyone else's in our family of four. If their rooms were downstairs, I was upstairs. If their rooms were upstairs, I was down. During those years, I felt pushed to the side.

Looking back, I can see my parents' choices had to do with logistics. My younger brother was four years younger than me. Of course he'd always have the room closest to our parents. Yet what may have been common sense to everyone else felt like abandonment to me. They were together. I wasn't. A seed of abandonment had been planted early in my life and watered by circumstances.

Good Enough

Growing up, I wondered why my biological dad didn't ever come to see me. I tried to be good enough so he would. I always tried to behave, and I never got into trouble. I had no idea back then that he didn't know I existed.

My stepfather wasn't very interested in me, and when I entered my teen years, I looked for love in the wrong places. My first serious boyfriend—who I thought was my true love—moved away. The next serious boyfriend got me pregnant. As I mentioned previously, I chose to have an abortion because I feared what people would think of me. I didn't want my grandma to know what I'd been doing. Maybe I feared the people who loved me would abandon me, too, when they found out I'd been sexually active and was pregnant.

Even when my boyfriend treated me horribly or was dating other girls, I was angry because I wasn't the one cared for or chosen. I'd physically fight with these other girls. (Yes, really!) I hated them even more than I hated my boyfriend. He'd chosen them and not me.

When I got pregnant for the second time by that same boyfriend, he broke it off for good. Embarrassed and dealing with morning sickness, I dropped out of school. My friends didn't call. I was at the lowest of lows. The ache was a sharp pain in my chest. Thankfully, I turned to God, but the root of abandonment remained.

Even as an adult, when I considered finding my biological dad, I told myself that I needed to lose twenty pounds and have a book published first. I still felt I had to be good enough to be loved. When I finally reached out to my biological dad, I found out that I had four sisters, but his wife refused to let me meet them. That broke my heart.

When John and I took our three kids down to meet my biological dad for the first time, he acted as if he was going to work, and he wore a business suit to the zoo so his wife wouldn't know he was meeting up with us. I felt he was a coward for not standing up for himself and for me.

I wish I could say that this root of abandonment has been uprooted, but it's still something God and I are working on.

Emotions Point to Areas That Need Healing

When my children were little, sometimes they would get so upset that there was no consoling them. They would cry and cry until they were emotionally spent. They would fall into a restless sleep because they were exhausted, physically and emotionally. That's how I feel when these emotions (which I now know to be shades of abandonment) hit.

The emotions emerge quickly, pulling everything from me. I've told my husband before that when these emotions come, I feel like someone has plugged a device into me and then drained me dry. I can imagine where the root started: a little toddler wrapped in her grandma's arms, crying for her mother until there were no more tears left. The heart remembers even when the mind does not.

It makes sense, doesn't it? I was lying in a bed, curled in a fetal position, when I accepted Christ. I'd come to the end of myself and needed Him. The toddler felt alone, but the teen knew enough about the Living God to make a good choice. When I find myself in that situation now, the adult now knows that these emotions stem from a heart of abandonment. I now understand why I feel as I do.

Logically, I can think through each of these situations and understand that no one meant to make me feel abandoned. Yet each time I've felt these "betrayals" in the past, I went to bed and tucked myself in. I didn't want to see anyone. I wanted to sit in my pain, cry, and be alone. But after a while, when I realized that pulling away wasn't helping, I turned to God's Word, allowing it to bring peace.

Contemplating these emotions and reactions—and the root of abandonment—has brought me peace. Seeing where the source of abandonment has come from has helped me understand myself better. It's given me something to take to God, and we're still working through this together.

Soul Care for Our Inner Lives

As I mentioned in an earlier chapter, "soul" is the most common translation of the Hebrew word *nephesh* and the Greek word *psyche*. The biblical meanings of these concepts are extremely rich. In the Old Testament, the definitions of *nephesh* range from "life," "the inner person (particularly thoughts, feelings, and passions)," to "the whole person, including the body." The soul distinguishes humans from animals and living from dead. It is also the source of emotions, will, and moral actions.

Similarly, in the New Testament, *psyche* carries such meaning as the totality of a person, physical life, mind, and heart. Here, the soul is the religious center of life and the seat of desire, emotions, and identity. Many biblical scholars suggest that the best single word for both *nephesh* and *psyche* is either "person" or "self." The great advantage of such an understanding is that both words carry the connotation of wholeness. Self is not a part of a person, but their totality.[1]

To tend to our souls is to care for the center of ourselves. To do this, we must pay attention to our inner lives. While I do remember to eat and sleep, I often forget my soul needs nourishment and rest.

I walk through my day with rituals of work, caring for family, and tending my home. Too often, I don't nurture my interests, seek to care for myself, or clean up the messes that pile up in my mind and heart—like the root of abandonment. Yet when I don't take care of my inner life, it's usually apparent in my exterior life. When something painful hits, I'm knocked off my feet. Or, more specifically, sent to my bed in a fetal position.

Soul Care Often Means Engaging with People for Help

God uses other people to tend to our souls. We need to engage in relationships. We can be intentional by reaching out to safe friends and letting them know our struggles.

I was having a tough time in my life due to challenges with my teenage kids. The burdens physically weighed on me in the form of high blood pressure that forced me to get on medication.

I knew I needed help, so I sought out a Christian counselor. I pictured something like what you see in movies: lying on a couch and pouring out my problems while my counselor listened sympathetically. But my counseling was nothing like that. I had barely shared a fraction of what was going on when he started directing me to find solutions. At first, I didn't like it. I wanted to wallow in the unfairness of all that was happening, but he urged me to consider changes I could make to resolve some of the problems in my life.

My counselor wasn't the only one. I have a dear friend who is also a counselor. She called to check on me, and I started going into all my struggles. "Well, Tricia," she said, "it's just time to put your big-girl panties on and get out of bed and deal with it." Her words shocked me, but I did just that. I got out of bed and started dealing with it the best I could. The first way I dealt with it was by accepting that hardships are just a part of life. Believe it or not, accepting that is soul care, too.

Soul Care Means Accepting Hardships

During these hard times over the last few years, I got miffed at God for bringing such hardship into my life. Many emotions surfaced during this time, and the first step to dealing with them was to accept them. Hiding my ache didn't help one bit. We can only attempt to stuff our feelings down for so long. I had to admit that this root of abandonment made me feel as if God had also abandoned me.

Can you relate? Have you ever felt abandoned by God? Maybe, like me, you never paused to really consider the losses you've faced. Looking back on your life, you might feel as if you were the problem, instead of seeing loss as a natural part of life. Abandonment isn't so much about the situation; it's how we perceive the situation. If you were a child, you may not have clearly understood what was really going on. Children tend to internalize events around them. Little ones often feel as if they are at fault for losses in their lives, when that's not the case at all. Sadly, we continually carry these emotions of abandonment with us, and additional hard circumstances or losses through life cause the chasm of pain to widen and deepen inside us.

Maybe, like me, you'll benefit from really thinking through your feelings and where they stem from. Hopefully this contemplation can bring clarity and peace to your soul. Even now, I have to remind myself to really look at the situation and not immediately allow feelings of abandonment to wash over and paralyze me. When the ache stirs, I'm learning to step away for a moment to ask, "What's really going on?" And sometimes this means stepping away again and again, especially in more difficult or ongoing situations.

For months, I questioned why God opened my heart and John's toward adoption. Why? The circumstances with some of our kids cut me to the core. I didn't like how I was treated. I didn't want to see John and the other kids hurt, either. I wrestled with the question, "Why do bad things happen when you're following God?" And through my wrestling, I came to a few conclusions:

1. I don't see the end picture, and good is still possible.

I hoped that I was in the painful middle and that good would come from the bad. I still do.

2. God never promised that life would be perfect.

In fact, throughout the Bible, God's followers are told they will suffer. 2 Timothy 1:8 says:

> So never be ashamed to tell others about our Lord. And don't be ashamed of me, either, even though I'm in prison for him. With the strength God gives you, be ready to suffer with me for the sake of the Good News.

At its core, adoption is caring for children as parents and raising them to know the Lord. Yet the Good News isn't always accepted, even within one's home.

3. I wrongly expected that because I followed God, He would reward me.

As a gold-star-loving girl, I have always strived for the A (and any extra credit). Yet there have been days I felt my role as a mother earned me a big fat F. I had to remind myself that my thinking was wrong.

4. I (also wrongly) believed that if I hadn't adopted kids with traumatic backgrounds, life would be easier.

There is no guarantee of this, of course. Trouble comes to all of us as long as we're alive. It's easy to picture the comfortable, easy, empty-nester life that I never got to have, but what guarantee was there that John would have the excellent job he has? Or that I would still be writing and publishing books? Or that we wouldn't have health problems or financial issues? By choosing to adopt kids, I didn't give up an "easier" life. Since this is God's direction, I must believe that this is the right path, even with challenges.

Even though the root of abandonment has been at play in my life, there's something else going on: I've also struggled with feelings of worth. As a child, I believed that my biological dad would come to see me if I was good enough. And as an adult, I've felt the same way about God.

Even though I received beautiful messages about God's love and the salvation found in Christ, I also picked up many beliefs about the "right" way to be a Christian. I struggled with becoming heart happy for many years because, deep down, I felt I wasn't doing enough. Our feelings of worth are tied to happy hearts. If we're always trying to do more, we'll never settle down enough to allow God to connect with our hearts.

The "Right" Way to Be a Christian?

I am so thankful to have grown up in a small country church. I clearly remember the scratchy pews and hardback hymnals. I have fond memories of sitting in the fourth row on the left with my grandparents and mom. I cherished the smiling saints of that church, forever captured in my mind, the older people in the congregation who knew my name and always patted my head or squeezed my shoulder to say hello. The sermons were a mix of "Jesus loves you enough to die for you," and "You better live right or you're going to suffer." It was those types of "turn or burn" messages that perhaps caused me to struggle with feeling good enough, clean enough.

Up until five years ago, I was nervous every time we took communion. Why? Because I remember being told that before you took communion, you had better confess all your sins, lest sickness or even death come upon you. It wasn't until recently when I realized that worrying whether I remember every sin to confess isn't the point of communion. Instead, the issue is coming together to remember the body of Jesus broken and the blood of Jesus poured out on the cross for me.

Both messages took root in those pews: God loved me, but He would punish me if I sinned. That's why, when I became sexually active as a teenager, I stopped going to church and stopped thinking about God. I wanted to live my way, and I didn't want to think about His disapproval. Like if I didn't acknowledge Him, I wouldn't have to feel guilty or face His punishment. That continued for years—until I was so wholly depressed, alone, and broken that His love became a greater need than His wrath was a worry.

When I prayed, "God, I have screwed up big time. If You can do anything with my life, please do," the love, joy, peace, and light that flooded into my heart was overwhelming and beautiful. I haven't lived a perfect life since (not close!), but my thoughts about my value to God have changed.

I understand now that the don'ts in the Bible are there because God knows that following those paths will lead to pain and destruction. It's not that He's sitting around waiting to punish me, but rather He longs to protect me from desires that will lead to wrong choices and to shield me from the bad decisions that lead to internal and external brokenness.

I didn't get that growing up. It was more about rules than relationships. Learning more about God's heart through reading His Word has changed my thinking. Making a point to connect with Him every day—my spirit to His Spirit—and becoming heart happy has changed my feelings of worth, too.

God is for me. He is an ever-present help with whatever I need. He desires to give me wisdom if I ask. He's available for direction if I pause to acknowledge that He knows the way.

I've come to realize that God loves me more than I can imagine, and He has good plans for my life, so why wouldn't I want to seek Him? As I draw near to Him, I feel His love. As I feel His love, I am filled up, and my whole perspective on my day changes. No longer do I focus on trying not to sin. Instead, my mind is set on Him, and sin isn't even attractive.

I'm no longer worried about the "right" way to be a Christian. Instead, I long to love God and love others better, and somehow it all works out. Once we understand God better, we'll better understand His care for us. Knowing God's identity helps us to embrace ours. Yet to accept this, we have to stop hiding.

It's Time to Stop Hiding from God

Maybe you, too, have been hiding from God. We don't feel good enough, clean enough, so we run instead of facing Him. It's been this way from the beginning of time. Genesis 3:6 says:

> When the woman saw that the fruit of the tree was good
> for food and *pleasing* to the eye, and also desirable for

gaining wisdom, she took some and ate it. She also gave some to her husband, who was with her, and he ate it. (NIV, emphasis mine)

In Hebrew, "pleasing" is *tawah*, and it means "to intensely crave." "Desirable" in Hebrew is *khamadh*, and its definition is "to covet" or "to delight in." This can refer to proper delight and fondness as well as improper lust and desire.[2] Eve wanted wisdom and insight right that moment. She had an appetite that she couldn't deny. The thing was, Eve also walked daily with God, which points to intimacy and fellowship. Genesis 3:8 says, "Then the man and his wife heard the sound of the LORD God as he was walking in the garden in the cool of the day, and they hid from the LORD God among the trees of the garden" (NIV). Adam and Eve weren't surprised that God was there, but for the first time, they desired to hide because of their sin.

Eve's desire caused her to sin, and she lost intimacy with God. Through that intimacy, she could have gained insight and wisdom, according to God's timing. God could have been her trainer and teacher as she learned from Him. Instead, her craving led her to sin, and strife struck both Eve and her husband a hard blow. As Paul David Tripp writes, "Before sin is a matter of behavior, it is always a matter of the heart."[3] Instead of hiding, we need to discover the intimacy we desire in God. We need to draw close instead of running away. As Hebrews 4:16 says:

Therefore let us [with privilege] approach the throne of grace [that is, the throne of God's gracious favor] with confidence and without fear, so that we may receive mercy [for our failures] and find [His amazing] grace to help in time of need [an appropriate blessing, coming just at the right moment]. (AMP)

I believe that true confidence is a spiritual quality that fundamentally affects how we see the world, each other, ourselves, and God. The author of Hebrews says, "Now faith is *confidence* in what we hope for and assurance about what we do not see" (11:1 NIV, emphasis added). The word here that we translate as "confidence" is *hypostasis*, which literally means "the supporting structure," "the basis for something," "our assurance," or "strong understanding." It's the power under something that provides a foundation for what's above it. This definition helps explain why I see confidence as an essential quality in one's soul...our confidence supports our life's journey.

What happens when we're not confident? We hide from God. We feel abandoned. We feel unworthy. We question whether we measure up. Of course, these are not fun feelings, so we try to find worthiness in other ways. How? We try to make something of ourselves in our efforts. Then in doing so, we become completely exhausted. We try to catch up with all the things we believe we're to do as Christians, and then we fall flat on our faces. But it doesn't have to be this way. Trying to catch up keeps us from what we need most: intimacy with God.

Stop Trying to Get Caught Up

What do you think of when you hear the term "caught up?" For me, it's this idyllic place somewhere in the future where most of my work is finished, most of my chores are done, and where I can spend an afternoon going out to coffee with a friend or spending a few hours in a backyard hammock reading one of the novels on my huge to-read pile. Of course, I don't have a backyard hammock, and I rarely allow myself to take off an afternoon. I take time to go to coffee or lunch with friends, but usually, it's when I'm away speaking and don't have all the pressing commitments that come with being at home.

My guess is that your number one hindrance in taking time to draw close to God—and making your heart happy in the Lord—is that you don't have time. I understand. As a mom of ten, grandma of many, and wife, there is always someone who needs something from me.

I manage both a home and a business. I am a full-time home-schooling teacher and writer. I am responsible for my kids' education, and I write on average four books a year, in addition to speaking, blogging, and podcasting. If I were to work sixty hours a week (I don't!), I'd have something to fill every minute, and then I'd still have more.

My guess is that you feel the same. Maybe you're a mom who never feels as if she has one minute for herself. You thought things would get easier when your kids got older, but then came traveling and sports. Perhaps you're caring for an ailing family member or you're facing health struggles of your own. Maybe you're in a job you don't love, or you're waiting and praying for a spouse. Or perhaps everything seems okay in life, but you're dreaming of "something more." The truth is that you don't have to be a mom of ten to feel overwhelmed and worn out. It happens to all of us.

If we are honest, there will never be a time when we're caught up. And so we keep plugging forward and pouring out. We give more and more. Do more and more. Yet there will always be more to do. Always. But it doesn't help to do more if we don't do it from a happy heart. We feel empty because we're spinning our wheels and getting nowhere.

Whenever I'm asked my "secret to doing it all," I always land on this: I take time to be with Jesus. I spend time reading His Word and in prayer. I spend time in worship. I get my heart and mind focused on the right things, and then everything about the day works better. Having the right priorities, the right attitude, and correct motivations come from my time with Jesus. And they only happen when I make the time to nourish my soul.

Yes, Bible reading takes time, prayer takes time, worship takes time, rest takes time, choosing to be creative and enjoying your God-given gifts takes time—but I know from experience that this time is redeemed tenfold.

The worst thing you can do is try to "catch up" on all your numerous tasks before focusing on soul care. I promise you will NEVER catch up. Your work will never be complete—whether it is work inside the home or outside of it. When you finish that to-do list, there will be twenty more things you can immediately add.

When you take time for soul care and making your heart happy, you might discover that things you thought you needed to "catch up on" aren't priorities at all. As you spend time with God, your priorities might even shift to something completely different. (They probably will.) And because Jesus loves you and has good plans for you, the new priorities will most likely be the right ones, and they will lead you to an abundant life.

I can't tell you the number of times God has given me a new book idea—or a simple way to connect with a troubled child—as I've sought Him. Jesus has led me to beautiful, transforming changes when I've taken the time to spend with Him. Here are some things to take to heart when it comes to priorities:

1. We cannot let needs determine our pace.

There are real needs and there are perceived needs—and between them both, there will be more needs than we can meet alone. In my life, there are always one or two people who need help on any given day. This week alone, John and I talked through a job change with an adult child, helped teens think through dating issues, and assisted two other adult kids in moving, each forty-five minutes away from us in opposite directions! That's not counting daily homeschooling of my younger kids and caring for my ninety-two-year-old grandmother. And I'm sure you have your own list of people with needs and crises pulling you in 100 different directions, too.

The perceived needs swirl around my mind, too. Should I reach out more to my college-aged daughter? Should I offer to babysit so my son and his wife can go out on a date? Should I be reaching out to my neighbors more? The correct answer to all these things is yes, yes, and yes, because all those things are good. Yet, it comes to the point where I have to choose what to focus on today.

I've learned—after running myself to exhaustion numerous times—to choose a few things to focus on and then say, "That is enough. That is all I can do." I have to trust that the Lord will stir my heart when to reach out to my college-aged daughter, serve my older kids, and how and when to love my neighbors. Good things are only good when they flow naturally from our lives and not because we worry we aren't doing enough or feel guilty. Worry and guilt should not be part of our decision-making process.

2. We should not stay busy for fear of slowing down.

It's easy to get addicted to busyness. Sometimes we can even get an adrenaline boost by helping others. But we can only keep going for so long. Taking more naps, getting our nails done, and having dinner around the table with our families are all good things, but they don't go spirit-level deep. That takes grounding ourselves in God.

Keeping busy is also a tactic we use when we want to avoid our emotions. It's easy to keep ourselves busy rather than processing what's going on in our hearts, lives, and world. Even though it's exhausting, volunteering to help a friend or serving someone in need takes less emotional energy than sitting still and processing heart issues like abandonment. Yet this is why we need to sit still before God. Not only do we need to process our emotions and thoughts, but we need to do so in light of God's Word.

I can be heartbroken by the choices of one of my kids. I can even question if I'm doing enough as a mom or if any of my efforts matter at all, but as I sit down with Jesus, His Word reminds me, "Whatever you did for the least of these brothers and sisters of mine, you did for me" (Matthew 25:40 NIV).

When I hear about a tragic world event or question the moral depravity that attempts to draw my children away from God's truth, the Bible reminds me, "In this world you will have trouble. But take heart! I have overcome the world" (John 16:33b NIV).

Our bodies/minds/spirits can't keep going nonstop. Just as our bodies need to sit down and take a breather, our minds and souls do, too. As we sit before God, our strength is renewed.

"Soul care requires that we slow down, because our pace of life likely prevents us from asking questions and facing traumatic realities," writes Bethany Dearborn Hiser in her book *From Burned Out to Beloved*.[4] As Isaiah 40:30–31 says:

> Even youths grow tired and weary, and young men stumble and fall; but those who hope in the LORD will

renew their strength. They will soar on wings like eagles; they will run and not grow weary, they will walk and not be faint. (NIV)

3. We need to break free from the busy lifestyle the world promotes.

Romans 12:2 says:

Do not conform to the pattern of this world, but be transformed by the renewing of your mind. Then you will be able to test and approve what God's will is—his good, pleasing and perfect will. (NIV)

The pattern of this world is to keep striving to do better and achieve more. That is not God's good, pleasing, and perfect will. God's kingdom isn't about "more"; it's about "enough." Ecclesiastes 4:6 says, "Better one handful with tranquility than two handfuls with toil and chasing after the wind" (NIV).

Even as I reread this verse, I can picture where I was sitting in my living room, with the early morning sun peeking through the windows, as I read those words years ago and felt the burden of "doing enough" lift off my shoulders. The truth of the Scriptures stilled me even as the shouts of the world declared, "You're not doing enough!" Over the last twenty years, I've turned to this Scripture repeatedly to remember that my value is not based on doing more.

This idea of value directs our lives. We want to appear accomplished, compassionate, and in step with the world around us without really pausing long enough to listen to our heart scream, "Enough! This has to stop. There really are issues going on that we need to discuss." More than being worried about missing deadlines or feeling left out, the deeper issue is, "Am I enough?"

If we take time to get quiet with Jesus, we will find the answer. The questions that cause us to keep striving can only be answered by the One who truly loves us most and best. But we must be willing to listen as Jesus speaks to our hearts about our value.

Going Deeper

We often focus on doing the external because we are unsettled in the internal. Our identity is based on what we do rather than who we are. We may get validation by our works, yet everything changes when we understand our value.

We can be called without being crushed. We can be compassionate to others while also giving compassion to ourselves. We can pray about others' needs—and trust in God's provision—without trying to fix all their needs in our own strength.

One of the things that changed my life most was seeing myself through God's eyes of love rather than being worried about what I accomplish or what others think about me. In the words of Ephesians 1:4–5:

> Even before he made the world, God loved us and chose us in Christ to be holy and without fault in his eyes. God decided in advance to adopt us into his own family by bringing us to himself through Jesus Christ. This is what he wanted to do, and it gave him great pleasure.

God appreciates when we serve others' needs, but we often serve to prove our own value. However, when we already understand how valuable we are to God, we don't need to strive to get our kudos elsewhere. For example, knowing I'm the one who brings our family together around the dinner table every night—fostering our connections and nourishing our bodies—I enjoy planning meals and cooking. My motivations are internal for the most part. (Yes, I do enjoy the excellent food, too!) Yet if I cooked with external motivations—such as my family applauding my efforts and exuberantly showing their gratitude, I'd be sorely discouraged most nights.

If I cooked for "thank-yous" alone, I'd feel discouraged, exhausted, and defeated. Fortunately, my motivations go deeper. I know my kids will look back on times around the dinner table with fondness, even if they don't understand that yet. I know the simple, everyday meals that I cook will be ones they ask for when they visit home as adults because of their familiarity and enjoyment.

I know this because when my daughter visits from Europe, she asks for tuna casserole—yes, the kind with tuna, noodles, sour cream, and cream of mushroom soup. That casserole will never win any culinary awards, but it feels like home to her. I know that now, and that internal motivation fuels me even when the kids around my table are focused more on finishing their food and getting back to their play than giving me kudos for my hard work.

Everything changes when we understand our value and true motivations. If I depend on my family to meet all my needs, I'll be disappointed time and time again.

"Our inner beliefs and perceptions affect our care for others and ourselves," writes Bethany Dearborn Hiser in her book *From Burned Out to Beloved*:

The beliefs we hold about ourselves can drive us to burnout. Without our awareness, false beliefs drive our feelings of anger, shame, guilt or unworthiness. We end up less able to care for the person in front of us and more likely to be depleted due to stress and lack of rest...Understanding our beliefs is an important step to free us from shame and to help us move toward wholeness and resilience.[5]

Knowing our value flows from the happy heart we feel within—not from striving to feel better. When we know our worth, we can offer ourselves to others without conditions of what we'll get back in return. We have not been abandoned. We do not have to feel as if we measure up. Instead, we can draw close to God and begin to understand how He sees us and how He has created us to impact the world, not due to our striving, but due to the natural outflow of our relationship with Him.

Your Turn

We often are confused by who God is, yet when we understand His grace and compassion—even in the daily stuff of life—we will desire to turn to Him often, tend our souls, and cultivate a happy heart throughout the day.

Get out your journal and begin to answer these questions for yourself. The important thing is not to give the Sunday School answer. Instead, take time to think through what your heart believes and why.

Who is God?

What is God like?

What does God want from me?
How does God relate to me?
What is God's purpose for me?
Does God love me—like, really?

---

5 Minutes to Connect

Write out Ephesians 1:4–5:

> Even before he made the world, God loved us and chose us in Christ to be holy and without fault in his eyes. God decided in advance to adopt us into his own family by bringing us to himself through Jesus Christ. This is what he wanted to do, and it gave him great pleasure.

Next, go through each phrase of these verses and turn to God in a prayer. You can pray prayers of thanksgiving or prayers of direction. You can pray for understanding and for truth. Also, ask God to help you understand your true worth in His eyes.

CHAPTER EIGHT

Being Compassionate to Others and Ourselves
Accepting True Grace

The LORD is gracious and righteous; our God is full of compassion.

Psalm 116:5 NIV

In my life, there have been a few key moments when I was going one direction, but God's Spirit stirring within my heart caused me to head another way. One of those was when I was a young, homeschooling mom who was just starting to get published in magazines. Knowing my past of having an abortion at age fifteen and becoming a teen mom at seventeen, our pastor asked if I'd be interested in helping start a crisis pregnancy center. When I sat down to pray about it the next day, I was genuinely asking God to show me how to tell Pastor Daniel that I didn't have time to launch a ministry.

As I sat with an open Bible in my lap and my eyes closed in prayer, a thought filled my mind. *What about the young women who are facing the fear and worry that you once faced? What are you going to do to help them?*

God's voice wasn't audible, but I knew the thought that filtered in was from Him. My answer had been, "Uh, no, I don't have time for this."

God's whisper stirred compassion that has impacted me for twenty years. That ministry did launch, and for most of the ensuing two decades, I mentored young moms.

Compassion grew as God called me to look beyond my home, family, and dreams. Through this compassion, thousands of young moms have received encouragement through the support groups I've led and through the book *Teen Mom: You're Stronger Than You Think* (2015), which followed.

Yet as I grew in compassion for others, I forgot to be compassionate with myself, which has been a significant detriment to my soul. It's far easier for me to look at another woman and see that she needs help and hope, information and inspiration, care and compassion. But it is hard for me to realize this for myself. Part of this stemmed from my "why." Even though God had called me to serve young women, I continued to do it far beyond my capacity to make up for my own feelings of unworthiness. Maybe you understand. What have you continued to do that was beyond your capacity because you felt unworthy or because you felt you needed to please someone else? Perhaps there is more than one thing.

As a young mom, I tried to have the perfect little Christian family because I knew how much I'd messed up as a teen, and I longed to do things differently—better. Also, how dare I not offer myself, my home, my life to others when God had given me so much?

Some of us also may withhold compassion from ourselves as a form of self-inflicted punishment. Guilt whispers:

You know what you did . . . now it's time to make up for those wrongs.

Look at you. You have so much when they have so little. How can you be so greedy? How can you not give more?

You can rest after your work is done. People are counting on you.

All these thoughts have entered my mind, and all of them have pushed me toward doing more and more without stopping to give myself rest. Yes, there are things that God calls us to, but it's important to know how much we should give. Every time I saw a need, I'd offer help, even as I grew weary in trying to keep up.

For many years, I also felt guilty if I sat still, especially when there was so much work around the house. My Hispanic grandmother and mother had modeled how to care for a home and family. Things were done a certain way. There was a home-cooked meal every evening. Laundry never piled up. After being washed, clothes were ironed and then hung in closets. The house was always clean. Never mind that my mother only had two children, not ten. And never mind that my grandmother was retired. They'd set a standard, and I felt I'd fallen short if I didn't reach it.

After adopting seven children in five years, I exhausted myself trying to keep up. More mouths to feed, clothes to wash, fights to break up, appointments to hold, and therapies to administer. More kids who needed me, bringing me to exhaustion.

After an especially overwhelming day, I crumbled to my knees in my laundry room. Tears filled my eyes as I stared at the mountain of dirty clothes before me "God, I can't do this," I said. I didn't have one more ounce to give.

The response from God that filtered into my mind surprised me.

I love you just as much with all the clothes piled up as I do if you're all caught up. His voice was a gentle, compassionate whisper to my soul.

That one phrase whispered to my spirit opened the door to me giving compassion to myself, too. If God can love me and be pleased with me when there are piles of laundry, can I love and be happy with myself, too?

Struggling with Self-Compassion

If a person is compassionate toward others, it does not necessarily mean they are compassionate with themselves or that others will be compassionate toward them. Compassion and self-compassion differ in nature and purpose. Most people tend to feel more compassion for others than for themselves. Yet more self-compassionate people have fewer depressive symptoms, fewer negative emotions, and more positive emotions. When we are compassionate to ourselves and realize it's good for us to slow down and connect with God, our feelings will change for the better.[1]

"We can learn to love ourselves as we love our neighbors," writes Bethany Dearborn Hiser. "This is a journey of pride and brokenness, of learning to say no and asking for help."[2]

God's Word speaks of this, too. Colossians 3:12 says, "Therefore, as God's chosen people, holy and dearly loved, clothe yourselves with compassion, kindness, humility, gentleness and patience" (NIV). Why should we demand more from ourselves than God demands from us?

Why should we insist on perfection when God declares, "Come to Me, all who are weary and heavily burdened" (Matthew 11:28, AMP)?

We're not doing ourselves any favors by withholding self-compassion. Sometimes this means releasing our high standards for things that don't matter in the long run—like always being caught up on laundry or never going to bed with dishes in the sink. There's a balance. I cannot say yes to every need. Sometimes, when I'm following God's call, I need to remember it's impossible to do everything perfectly all the time.

When I'm compassionate with myself and recognize my weaknesses, I'm more empathetic toward others. As I set limits and seek to care for myself, I'm more understanding to others who need to do the same. As I affirm my value, I better see the value of others. As I decide to seek God's best for me, I long to teach others to do the same. It all starts with compassion.

Self-Compassion Is Soul Care

My greatest act of self-compassion came when I forgave myself for having an abortion. My selfishness had inflicted pain and loss. I took a child's life. I was to blame. Even after confessing my sin and asking Jesus to forgive me, I had a hard time forgiving myself. If I forgave myself, would that mean I didn't accept the seriousness of my choice?

We cannot feel or show genuine compassion to someone without forgiving them, and that is true of ourselves, too. I decided to forgive myself when I realized I had been scared and groping around in the darkness, trying to find a way out and choosing the wrong one.

I made a choice then that I would not make today with the light of Jesus guiding me. I had to choose to be compassionate to that scared, overwhelmed teen. I also had to understand that Jesus was there, too, having compassion on me and loving me, even when I refused to come to Him or accept His love.

Forgiving myself—and choosing to love myself—was a cataclysmic moment of self-compassion, but I have to make smaller choices daily, too. As a human, I will mess up. Simple mistakes happen. We don't need to hold it against ourselves. We don't need to inflict punishment when we miss a deadline, speak harshly to a friend, or gain the ten pounds back that we just worked so hard to lose. Instead, we need to seek forgiveness, make better choices, and move on. Self-inflicted punishment or self-destructive thoughts will get us nowhere. We need to embrace the truth of God's mercy and grace for our sins and our mistakes. Psalm 103:8–12 says,

> The LORD is compassionate and merciful, slow to get angry and filled with unfailing love. He will not constantly accuse us, nor remain angry forever. He does not punish us for all our sins; he does not deal harshly with us, as we deserve. For his unfailing love toward those who fear him is as great as the height of the heavens above the earth. As far as the east is from the west, so far does he remove our transgressions from us.

"When we treat others with respect and caring, the best in them usually comes out," writes Rick Hanson, PhD, in his book *Resilient*. "Much the same would happen if we could treat ourselves the same way."[3]

Exhaustion is not proof you are loving well. I grew in self-compassion when I admitted that my wounded children were bringing pain to our home and my heart. Yes, they had been through more than any child ever should have to go through, but the pain they were inflicting on me was more than any parent—any person—is expected to handle. A parent shouldn't have to walk on eggshells around her home. A parent shouldn't shrink back in fear that there's going to be an explosion of anger when a child enters the room. I'm not sure why it took me so long to understand that.

Over the years, John and I have found resources to help our children. Things have greatly improved for our kids still at home. Some of our other children reached adulthood and chose to do things their own way in places beyond our home. We still love them, even when they've chosen different paths than we hoped for them.

Over the years, I've learned to tell myself, "You've done all you could. You've given all you were able, and now it's time to heal." Healing has come as I've tended my soul. Healing has come as I've grown in compassion for myself. Healing has also come as I've turned to God's compassionate heart.

God's Compassionate Heart

Sometimes, to truly understand God's heart, we need to read and re-read Scripture truths that highlight His compassion. These are a few of my go-to verses:

- When [Jesus] saw the crowds, he had compassion on them because they were confused and helpless, like sheep without a shepherd. (Matthew 9:36)
- So he returned home to his father. And while he was still a long way off, his father saw him coming. Filled with love and compassion, he ran to his son, embraced him, and kissed him. (Luke 15:20)
- But you, O Lord, are a God of compassion and mercy, slow to get angry and filled with unfailing love and faithfulness. (Psalm 86:15)

- The faithful love of the LORD never ends! His mercies never cease. Great is his faithfulness; his mercies begin afresh each morning. (Lamentations 3:22–23)
- He heals the brokenhearted and bandages their wounds. (Psalm 147:3)

The more I understand God's compassionate heart, the more empathetic I am toward others and myself. I prayed that God would "break my heart with the things that break His" while forgetting how brokenness feels. I'm starting to understand that, just as I placed heavy burdens on myself, I also put them on others by having unrealistic expectations for my family members and friends.

I should never have expected that children from trauma wouldn't have issues—or that I would be able to overcome all their pain with my love.

I shouldn't have tried to hold everything inside instead of sharing how challenging my situation was.

I should have understood that it's okay to go to God with my troubles again and again. God is not only OK with that; He longs to show His compassion to us.

Isaiah 30:18 (AMP) says,

Therefore the Lord waits [expectantly] and longs to be gracious to you, and therefore He waits on high to have compassion on you. For the Lord is a God of justice; Blessed (happy, fortunate) are all those who long for Him [since He will never fail them].

My soul is happy—it feels blessed and fortunate when I know that the Lord is there, waiting to show me compassion. I don't have to worry that I'm going to God too many times. I don't have to be ashamed when I am weak. God wants to help. He loves me and longs to be gracious to me. He wants to have compassion for me. He wants me to long for Him, to need Him.

Maybe you need to hear this, too: God still loves you entirely, even if you aren't meeting every need of those around you. He loves you because of who you are, not just because of what you do. It's impossible to meet every need. Jesus spoke to the crowds, yet He also stepped away to focus on individuals. Jesus withdrew to rest and pray. He sought to be strengthened, and only afterward could He pour out again.

Jesus modeled the type of life we need to live. Yet He was not just an example for us; He continues to be available to us. Proverbs 18:10 says, "The name of the LORD is a strong fortress; the godly run to him and are safe." Sometimes we forget amid our worry and pain that He is enough—turning to Him and running to Him is enough. Yet sometimes before we run to Him, we must be willing to call to Him.

Calling on God for Help

Do you struggle with calling to God for help? You shouldn't. Psalm 18:6 says,

> In my distress [when I seemed surrounded] I called upon the LORD and cried to my God for help; He heard my voice from His temple, and my cry for help came before Him, into His very ears. (AMP)

When was the last time you felt surrounded? In my everyday life, I am surrounded by people, by messes, and by projects. I'm also surrounded by noise, by the "stuff" of nearly a dozen people, and by my to-do lists. I can manage all these things—until I can't. If one of my kids makes wrong choices, or our plans are waylaid because of a crisis, my heart gets discouraged. All that surrounds me seems too much.

Some days I can pull away and give myself time to recover, but there are more days when I can't. In the middle of a thirty-two-hour drive toward a vacation destination, I can't get away for alone time. When there's baseball practice and older kids who need a ride to work, I can't hide in my bedroom for an hour to rest, read Scripture, and listen to worship music. But no matter what is happening, I can call on the name of Jesus.

Jesus, I need you.

Jesus, be with me now.

Jesus, be with my child.

Jesus, I need strength, hope, peace.

Jesus, have compassion on me.

Jesus, show me how to have compassion for myself.

Jesus.

These days, I call out to Jesus more than ever because I understand that it's OK to do so. No, more than that—it's *right* to do so. I have compassion on myself. I understand that Jesus has compassion for me. He loves me. I mean, He *really loves* me. (I'm smiling as I type this.) Jesus's desire is to connect with my heart, not just give me a list of things to do for Him. God sees me as His child, not His servant.

Some days, with compassion, I step out to help and love those in my community. My actions are an outpouring of love—love that stems from allowing Jesus to love me.

When I call out to Jesus, He delights in coming to me for connection. When I feel His love, when I get a glimpse of His heart, and when I understand His ways, my heart is made happy. I've always been blessed, but now my heart knows it. A happy heart is the result of realizing who I am and who loves me. My scattered thoughts are pulled in and can focus on the things that I forget: how much I am loved, how many good plans God has designed for me, how much compassion Jesus has for me, and the ever-present help of Jesus in every single aspect of my life.

Going Deeper

Your children and friends will learn more by watching how you move through this world with a happy heart than all those things they see you doing out of duty. Your children will learn to have compassion for others and for themselves when they see you modeling it.

Pause and consider the type of relationship with God that you want your children to have. If you could imagine a healthy spiritual life for them, what would that look like? What types of activities would you like to see your children involved in? What things do you hope your children will do in their lives? Now, if your child's only role model for living this type of life is you, would he or she be able to learn to live this way?

I don't bring this up to cause regret, guilt, or shame. That's the last thing I want to do! Instead, I hope these questions will encourage you to examine your life—just as I've had to examine mine.

What do you need to *stop doing* in order to grow in your relationship with Jesus and become heart happy? What do you need to *start doing* instead? And when I say "do," I mean things that foster soul care—which might mean stopping a lot of things that drain and overwhelm you in your efforts to "be a better Christian."

Consider how learning to have more compassion for yourself will wonderfully guide your children, too.

Your Turn

Take time to consider these questions:

1. How can I show myself compassion today?
2. What type of relationship with God do I wish for myself and my children?
3. What would a healthy spiritual life look like?
4. How can I model a life that is heart happy in the Lord?

5 Minutes to Connect

Create a list of compassionate affirmations you can use when you start to become too hard on yourself or find yourself striving to do more. I've started a list below. Add to it!

Whenever you need to be more compassionate to yourself, turn to these affirmations and remind yourself to call out to God.

- "I did what I thought was best then, but knowing more, I'm going to make different choices now with God's help."
- "I thought that would work but it didn't, so I'm going to try a new way."

- "I will do what I can today with compassion, and nothing more. It will be enough because God says I am enough."

CHAPTER NINE

Soul Care in the Midst of Suffering and Pain
Resilience

So we do not lose heart.
Though our outer self is wasting away,
our inner self is being renewed day by day.

2 Corinthians 4:16 ESV

Hard things will come, but soul care helps us to stand strong and bounce back when they do. Yet when we don't tend our soul, it's hard to be resilient. More than that, we get so fixed on Plan A (making everything better), we can't imagine a different way.

Although I am usually able to keep writing no matter the circumstances, last year I reached a point when I couldn't even open my email, let alone put together a string of thoughts for a book. I've always prided myself on being able to work in any condition, but I couldn't. I thought to myself, *This is it, I finally found my limit.*

My desire to fix my kids' broken places had broken me instead. Like shards of glass, the edges of their brokenness pointed outward in every direction. As John and I stepped forward to embrace our teens, offering love and belonging, their shards cut deeply into us.

Even worse than my pain, and John's pain, is theirs. My teen daughters lived through abuse, abandonment, and neglect from their earliest years. They had been removed from the only home they had known and moved from foster home to foster home. They'd been separated more than they'd been kept together. They'd been through a failed adoption. They'd been crushed to the point where they stopped hoping for good things to happen, because no good ever came from it when they did.

Even though our adoption didn't turn out as I wished, their lives hadn't turned out like they wanted either. Plan A hadn't worked; it was time for everyone to look for Plan B.

Plan B

We strive toward our own ideas, and we feel like failures when we don't achieve them. Because we want what's best, we often hold onto Plan A longer than we should. We work and work to help Plan A come to pass, even though it's impossible.

No matter how much I tried to help my teen daughters bond with us as parents, make good choices, and figure out safe and healthy plans for their futures, the older ones weren't going to have any of it. As I cried out tearfully to one of my adult sons, "I just want everyone to make good choices." The thing is, some people don't, and we can't force them to.

So I turned to a Christian counselor who listened, but quickly turned my mind to finding a Plan B. He reminded me that things didn't have to stay the way they were. Since our most difficult teen was nearly eighteen, he encouraged me to seek help for her outside of our home.

That was especially hard on me as a mom. I felt as if I'd failed my daughter who'd run to especially destructive choices, because all my love and all the therapy couldn't change her heart. I also felt I had failed our other family members because of what they witnessed due to her outbursts. I felt guilty that Plan A hadn't worked and guilty because I'd stuck to it for so long. Yet I knew things had to change, and the counselor gave me hope.

First, he told me about other young people who were able to build good relationships with their parents after they'd left home, and this gave me hope. I wanted to believe that our relationship with our daughter wouldn't always have to be so hard.

Second, he taught me that no matter how challenging things were, we could make changes. This involved putting our daughter into a residential treatment home for a while. She was able to get the intense counseling she needed, and we were able to get a bit of respite.

Our Plan B has changed a few times, because trying to steer someone in a good direction *outside* of our home has been just as difficult as trying to make her behave right *inside* of it. Recently, she chose to leave an amazing Christian program that we helped her get into. Instead, she's been bouncing between living with her biological mom and others whom we've never met. Now that she's an adult, she'll have to be the one who figures out what's next. It's truly out of my hands.

But the fact that I've accepted that is a victory for me. I'm learning to hold my plans loosely (whether they are A, B, or C), especially when they are dependent on other people's choices.

I can pray for all my children, and I can release them to God. I know that even if my children choose destructive paths, God loves them and wants good for them.

God knows that His Plan A—Himself—is the only place my children will be content and satisfied. Even as I'm hoping that my children will make good choices, my biggest prayer is that God's Plan A will win out. It may not be today or next year, but I will continue to pray that all my children choose God.

Refuge and Boundaries

Pain doesn't just come when we are physically ill or injured; it also can come with mental anguish. Facing heartbreak is a very real thing that can cause physical pain within us.

Suffering is both a mental and emotional challenge. Suffering comes with disappointment, anxiety, guilt, shame, loneliness, feelings of emptiness, and fears. Mental pain is no less real than other types of pain we face. It can also bring suffering.

Suffering can be present even without physical pain. An athlete might have pain as she trains, but she knows that the pain is for her greater good. Yet sometimes we can see no good in our suffering.

Through my suffering, I was able to connect with God in new ways. Because my Plan A didn't work, I was willing to look to God. I was broken down and had nothing to offer, yet God still loved me. I had always tried to earn love, but there was nothing I could do—nothing I could give—and yet God was still there. He not only hovered close, He didn't mind my questions. In fact, it was when I allowed myself to be completely vulnerable that I grew closer to God. I learned to trust Him even as I hated being a tangled mess of emotions and doubts. There were days I couldn't believe that anything good would come out of our experiences, but I finally got to the place where I trusted that God still loved me and that I still loved Him—and that was enough.

When I relinquished my life to Jesus as a pregnant teen, I believed I could be loved by God no matter *what I did*—that He would never give up on me. But during this later hard season of life, I learned I could be loved by God no matter *how I was*. I could come to Him as a complete emotional mess and that was OK, too.

Even when we are assaulted by pain and suffering, we can find a sense of heart happiness when we take refuge in the Son of God. When I am suffering due to the outbursts of an adopted child who's faced trauma, I can turn to God and find refuge. I can look to the greater good of being obedient as I care for the orphans and the widows. I can find communion, knowing that Christ also had people He loved who lashed out at times—like Mary and Martha, who were angry when Jesus didn't come quickly enough to keep Lazarus from dying, as reported in John 11.

Psalm 2:12 says, "All who take refuge in him are happy" (CSB). According to Strongs, the Hebrew word for *refuge* means "to flee for, protection, to confide in." We might have times in our lives when we need physical protection or healing from pain, but daily we can turn to God as refuge for our suffering. We can confide in Him with the pain that pierces our hearts. We can ask Him to protect us from becoming hard or bitter. Seeking refuge starts with admitting we are weak. It also means setting healthy boundaries.

Many years ago, when my grandfather passed away, we had to take a thousand-mile drive with a very difficult family member to his memorial service. This older family member is known for her sharp tongue. She is quick to point out everyone else's faults. It's hard enough dealing with her attitude and words in ordinary circumstances, but on top of the grief of losing my grandfather, it was just too much.

We'd barely gotten ten miles into our trip when this person started getting onto me about the funeral cards I'd created. She hadn't liked how they were done and was mad that I hadn't gotten her approval before printing them.

"Listen," my husband told her. "You need to stop now or I'm dropping you off at the nearest rest stop and you can find a way to get to the funeral from there."

Amazingly, my relative held her tongue for the next several hours—until we were about forty-five minutes from our destination. I suppose she figured we were close enough by then that she'd be able to call someone for a ride if need be. Then she said something else, and my husband gave her the same warning. That was enough for her to keep her lips sealed the rest of the way—and I learned something valuable from my husband's example. We can set clear boundaries. We do not have to be someone's punching bag, especially when we feel weak. Even in the midst of suffering, we get to choose how to respond.

During times of suffering, not everyone will be tender or caring with us. Sometimes we will need to put up boundaries to protect ourselves from others. Sometimes we also will need to put up boundaries so we can sift through how we're really doing. As hard as it can be, we can use our suffering to help us sort out what we're really thinking and feeling about ourselves, our situations, and about God.

Paying Attention

It's not easy to move from Plan A to Plan B. It's actually hard to go from trying to figure it all out ourselves to turning to God. One of the reasons for this is that we don't take time to pause and think about what's really going on. We think that if we just keep going, we can outrun the suffering. The thing is, that doesn't work. We need to pay attention to how we're feeling, and we need to allow ourselves to feel those emotions, even if it hurts.

Our emotions are signals. Negative emotions tell us that something's going on inside. It's important to take note of our emotions and discover what's triggering them. My friend and Christian counselor Jolene Underwood told me once, "When you name your emotion, there is an emotional release." Naming the emotions helps us to process them and take them to God. We can turn to Him and say, "I'm hurting, Lord. I'm sad. I'm angry."

The more I looked into this, the more I discovered so much truth in it. You can't change what you don't acknowledge. In a 2015 *New York Times* article titled "The Importance of Naming Your Emotions," Tony Schwartz wrote:

> So what's the value of getting people to express what they're actually feeling, rather than keeping things relentlessly light and bland? The answer is that naming our emotions tends to diffuse their charge and lessen the burden they create. The psychologist Dan Siegel refers to this practice as "name it to tame it."
>
> It's also true that we can't change what we don't notice. Denying or avoiding feelings doesn't make them go away, nor does it lessen their impact on us, even if it's unconscious. Noticing and naming emotions gives us the chance to take a step back and make choices about what to do with them.[1]

In my case, many of my hard emotions build when a small worry spirals out of control. Recently, I was struggling with one of my daughters who was not doing her schoolwork as she should. Every time I'd see her lying around, watching mindless videos instead of doing her homework, I'd flash ahead to next year to her NOT graduating. Seeing this, my blood pressure would rise, and I'd bear down on her. But instead of improving, she refused to change. More than that, she got worse.

I posted my frustration, in the form of a prayer request, on Facebook. Have you ever done that? One of my counselor friends called that night. "I could sense your tension in your post," Michelle said. "What's going on?"

After pouring out my justified frustrations, my friend said something unexpected. "She can only do what she can do. It sounds like she really struggles in school. She needs you to help her find ways to succeed. She needs to know what success looks like so she can duplicate it."

That wasn't what I wanted to hear. Instead of commiserating with me, my friend told me I needed to change. I needed to be more helpful and tender with my daughter. This message was confirmed the next morning during my devotions when I read, "Mercy means I am so deeply grateful for the forgiveness I have received that I cannot help offering the same."[2]

As one who usually underlines and highlights, I read the whole devotion, but I didn't highlight one word. To be honest, I wanted God to change my daughter and not me. I wanted a satisfactory answer without having to be involved in the solution. I wanted better results without putting in any work. Yet since the same message was coming to me in various ways, I knew I needed to pay attention.

I prayed for my daughter to grow up, to become responsible, and to change, but both my wise friend and God reminded me it was my job to become part of that process. Just as clearly as God had let me know that I needed to release my other daughter, I felt Him speaking with me to press in toward the one who was still at home and needing my help. It was through letting go and pressing in that I found resilience.

Resilience

We all face hardship, adversity, and stress, but even life-changing situations can make us stronger than before. Romans 5:3–5 says:

> And not only this, but [with joy] let us exult in our sufferings and rejoice in our hardships, knowing that hardship (distress, pressure, trouble) produces patient endurance; and endurance, proven character (spiritual maturity); and proven character, hope and confident assurance [of eternal salvation]. Such hope [in God's promises] never disappoints us, because God's love has been abundantly poured out within our hearts through the Holy Spirit who was given to us. (AMP)

The Greek word for "exult/rejoice" here means "to boast or vaunt." Another definition is "to brag."

I'll admit, it's not easy to brag about the hard things we go through—especially in the middle of them. Yet when we get to the other side, it's easier to see that the hardship has yielded good fruit. When we were growing up in church, we called this "giving a testimony." I still remember sitting in church in the early '80s and hearing the testimonies of those saved from a lifestyle of sex and drugs. During my speaking engagements, I often share the pain, heartache, and shame of being a teenage mom. I "boast" now because I can see that it took getting to my lowest low to finally dare to look up and find God there.

We can see a lot of change happening in Romans 5:3–5, and all of that inner change results from outer rejoicing. The endurance, character, hope, and assurance of our salvation are the result of a shift in our thinking. That shift happens when we are in the middle of a crisis and declare, "This hardship will strengthen me (give me endurance) and mature me (help me grow in character) as I depend *on* God (hope), knowing that I belong *to* God and He loves me."

When we face hardship, we often don't see our own resilience through it until we look back. I clearly remember being an overwhelmed and stressed mom of three kids. And then we adopted seven more children. Getting through each day got much harder, and when I look back at the things that used to stress me out before, they seem minor in comparison. I used to label my daughter Leslie as my "strong-willed one" until we adopted other kids that made her appear compliant by comparison.

When we face challenges, we can either become more resilient or we can crumble. Amazingly, our outcome comes down to our mind and heart.

In his book *Resilient*, Rick Hanson writes:

> There's a fundamental idea in psychology and medicine that the path your life takes depends on just three causes: how you manage your challenges, protect your vulnerabilities, and increase your resources.[3]

A perfect illustration of learning to be resilient happened when John and I went on a rafting trip with friends this summer. We had a wonderful guide, Wiggy, who knew the river well. As we quietly floated down a peaceful river, Wiggy told us we would face nine rapids ahead, and her job was to help us across the rough waters. She also told us that on most trips, at least one person finds themselves in the river. Even before we spotted the smallest ripple, Wiggy explained what to do if we fell into the water and what to do if we were the ones helping a friend back into the boat.

The words were barely out of her mouth when we came across the smallest ripples of whitewater. Truthfully, there is more foam in my bathtub than there was in the spot. Yet when we hit it, not one but TWO of the guys fell into the river. We hit the bump and *plop!* they were gone. Most of us were so shocked that we watched in stunned silence as one of the wives and Wiggy dragged our two soggy friends back into the boat.

After the shock came laughter, and Wiggy said those types of incidents are quite common the first time rapids are encountered. And the amazing thing was, no one was tossed into the water after that. The first bump was a shock, but it also prepared us for the rapids to come.

Resilience can be summed up in this way: It's the small dips in the river that best teach us to hold on and prepare for the rapids. When we face bumps in life, we learn to bounce back. As we learn to face challenges, we grow in endurance, character, and hope. We grow stronger and more assured.

All of us will face difficulty and distress, but what we do in the midst of those things makes the difference. According to the American Psychological Association, "Resilience isn't necessarily a personality trait that only some people possess. On the contrary, resilience involves behaviors, thoughts and actions that anyone can learn and develop."[4]

What helps us get through the bumps as we're building resilience?

1. Turning to understanding people.

When facing hardships with adoptive kids, I've found comfort when I've turned to other adoptive parents who understand what it's like. Just knowing that someone else has faced—or is facing—the same struggles allows me to share openly and builds a connection.

I've also reached out to a friend who's a counselor, and she often gives me insight or advice. She's pointed me to good resources, and she's reminded me to rest and care for myself. She's also encouraged me to get up and keep going when I've felt like giving up.

If you don't personally know anyone who can relate to your struggles, consider joining a support group. I'm part of an online support group for people caring for those with dementia. As I care for my grandmother, I find it helpful to hear from others who are going through the same thing. Even though I rarely ask questions, just reading the other posts helps. One person posted about getting a clock that says the day, month, year, and hour, and whether it is morning, afternoon, or night. This has helped with my grandmother, who sometimes calls out to me at 1:00 a.m. because she thinks it is 1:00 p.m. and time for lunch. Seeing others find positive solutions for problems like these helps me to see their resilience and to become more resilient myself.

2. Allow others into your hard spot, even if it feels uncomfortable.

One of the natural things to do when we face hardship and suffering is to isolate. I'll admit, I'm prone to that, too. After facing some especially hard struggles with our teen daughter, I texted a friend to update her on the situation. She asked if I needed her to come over. I told her I didn't, and then I climbed into bed and cried. Not fifteen minutes later, she walked into my bedroom.

"I told you I didn't need you to come," I told her.

"I know. But you lied," she said with a smile, and then sat on the end of the bed.

I sat up, wiped my tears, and we talked about what was happening. She listened and cared, and it was exactly what I needed. Her compassion pulled me out of my funk. When I wanted to pull away and drown in my sorrows, Deb tossed me a rope and pulled me out of the muck.

Even when we want to withdraw, one of the best things we can do is accept help and support. Being vulnerable is hard, but we need to remember that everyone needs help from others at times.

3. Look back at your previous hardships and consider what you learned and how you grew.

Recently, a pastor friend told me that he wouldn't trade being faced with divorce for a million dollars. That time helped him and his wife to strengthen their marriage and to rebuild their foundation on God. Another friend shared about her family's painful years planting churches overseas; the situation was so bad that it caused PTSD. Yet she says now she can see the fruit, and she's grateful for those who are continuing the work they started.

Looking back and taking note of your growth helps you see challenges in a new light. As I'm writing this, 2020 is still fresh in my thoughts. It was a challenge for everyone. No one expected having to pivot so much. All my speaking events were cancelled, which is a decent part of my income. But because of that, I learned how to put up and manage a web shop. I learned how to create and launch a course. I pumped out thirty-one self-published journals for kids in addition to writing two books. I also learned to paint in watercolor and cut hair! I have more skills now than before COVID, mostly because things did not go as planned and I had to learn to adjust.

4. *Keep things in perspective.*

It's important to stop yourself from worse-case-scenario thinking. Remind yourself that even big problems can be solved by making small changes. Also, it's helpful to remember that today's problems won't last forever.

5. *Set small goals.*

Ask, "What's one thing I know I can accomplish today that helps me move in the direction I want to go?"

A few years ago I was struggling with trying to homeschool seven children—four of whom had just been pulled out of public school and weren't used to the home environment or being around their siblings all day long (much less doing schoolwork side by side with them). I reached out to a friend who is a life coach, and she gave me great advice: "Write down what you would like your homeschool day to look like. Then write down small steps you can make to move that direction."

The first step was easy. I wrote, "I want to have a homeschool day where there are no big fights or tons of interruptions. Instead, I want everyone to get along and have fun learning together."

Small steps included giving my kids a full hour to wake up, eat, and get prepared for the day before making them all gather around the table. It involved making a list of school rules and going over them every day. I wrote down what correct behavior looked like. This included even obvious things like not calling each other names, raising our voices, or shouting out the answers to questions.

I also changed where everyone sat (because some personalities weren't clicking well), and I scheduled in more breaks and fun activities. Some things, such as the new seating arrangement, helped immediately, while others took more time.

But I remember the day, months later, when we had the home-school day I had always wanted: There were no fights, not too may interruptions, everyone got along, and we had fun learning together. I recognized the day because I was shooting for it. The kids recognized it, too, because they knew what we'd been working on and what we were striving for. We all grew in resilience as we worked together.

Sometimes we don't reach our goals because we haven't actually figured out what those goals are. We get down on ourselves for what's going wrong, but we don't take steps to figure out how to do things differently. We feel like we're stuck and sinking, yet we don't look around to see how to dig ourselves out—or better yet, how to find a better path that doesn't lead to quicksand. And that's why we need to take our goals back to God, daily spending time in His Word and prayer.

Everything changed in George Müller's life after he started conversing with God about what he read and then allowing prayer to flow naturally from that. As I did the same, my prayer of "God, help my daughter to be responsible," transformed into this:

"Lord, I would be in a miserable shape if You judged me for everything I've done wrong. I wanted my daughter to change with little effort on my part, but I know that instead of more restrictions, she needs more compassion and assistance. It doesn't matter what I was able to do at her age—she is a different person, and this is a different time. She faces more challenges in one day than I could ever imagine.

"Lord, I know You are asking me to help her. Forgive me for my lack of tenderheartedness and helpfulness. Help me today to be a cheerleader, inspiring her heart. Help me to remind her that she can turn to You for strength. You ARE available. Thank You for using the situation to teach me a better way. May my tender mercy impact our whole family. Also, show me other people who I need to be merciful toward."

Through learning about soul care, compassion, and paying attention, I have been changed. There is no one right answer for two different situations, and that's why it's important to turn to God. This is His Plan A for me, too. Turning to Him through all of my pain and suffering, understanding that He will have the right answers. He will see me through. Then, as change comes—internally, if not externally—I can start to hope.

Going Deeper

No matter how hard and painful things are, we can see beauty, seek possibility, and find ways to love life in the middle of our challenges, suffering, and pain. We can see the world through lenses of hope. Hope often starts when we change, or capture, our thoughts. Hope-vision can help us think of solutions when we're in the middle of problems and feel stuck.

God doesn't offer us freedom from a broken world; instead, He offers us friendship with Himself as we walk through a fallen world—and those who persevere will find that this friendship is worth more, so very much more, than anything we face. Even if we face it with tears.

Your Turn

Pray aloud or write out the reality of the pain that you're feeling because Plan A didn't work out. Confess the hurt, disappointment, confusion, and weariness of it all. Follow the example David took in writing so many of the Psalms. As you spill out your heart, end each thought with "yet I know..."

Lord, I am facing pain about _____. Yet, I know _____.

Lord, the heartache is too much because _____. Yet, I know _____.

Lord, there are no easy answers to _____. Yet, I know _____.

Lord, sometimes I feel alone in my suffering _____. Yet, I know _____.

5 Minutes to Connect

In this chapter I wrote, "I boast now because I can see that it took getting to my lowest low to finally dare to look up and find God there." Can you relate?

Take a minute to boast to God. Share all the low places you were and then boast about where He has taken you through His love and grace.

CHAPTER TEN

Finding Your Creative Refuge
The Steadfast Shelter of God

He will cover you and completely protect you with His pinions,
And under His wings you will find refuge;
His faithfulness is a shield and a wall.

Psalm 91:4 AMP

Have you ever heard the phrase, "She's her own worst enemy"? Hearing this, I think of someone who causes most of her own problems. When it comes to striving to *do more* and *be better,* our longings often lead us to this place. I'm my worst enemy when it comes to my schedule. My unrealistic expectations lead me to add more than is humanly possible, then I mentally beat myself up when I can't get everything done.

I'm my own worst enemy when I'm so busy doing things that I don't take time to enjoy life. I run from morning till night, and then I ask, "Isn't there more to life than this?"

I'm my worst enemy when I push aside time with God because I'm too tired to wake up or too unfocused to sit down and get anything meaningful out of God's Word.

I've been my worst enemy in all these situations, and dozens more, and the solution is seeking God's protection—not from outside influences, but from myself. I need to turn to God as my refuge. I need to discover who He uniquely created me to be.

When I pause to come to Jesus, I am covered with His love and I feel protected. Taking time to remember His love and sacrifice causes me to take in a deep breath, remembering that there is nothing I need to accomplish to earn a good reputation or a place in Heaven. I simply have to accept what Jesus has already provided for me through His sacrifice on the cross.

When I draw near to Jesus and find refuge, I know that who I am is enough. Jesus's tenderness toward me reminds me to be tender to myself. His faithfulness is a shield and a wall that keeps me from demanding more from myself than He does.

Perfect Peace

One of my favorite verses is Isaiah 26:3–4, "You will keep in perfect peace all who trust in you, all whose thoughts are fixed on you! Trust in the LORD always, for the LORD God is the eternal Rock." I love that phrase, "perfect peace," especially because in our busy, daily lives peace is often hard to find.

Our minds are quick to worry because we desire to keep ourselves safe. This is especially true if we've been impacted by trauma. We know bad things DO happen, and we may previously have been caught off guard. We believe that by worrying about bad things and preparing for them, we'll be better off. Yet this is never the case. By doing this, we are taking our current moments of peace and inserting worst-case scenarios, troubling our souls.

One of our teen daughters comes up with the craziest "what ifs," and presents them to me and John nearly every day. "If I was arrested, would you visit me in jail?" or "If the house was on fire, would you save me or the dog first?"

My response is often too logical. "Why don't we try NOT to get arrested?" and "Yes, I'd save you first, but if there is a fire, it's a good idea to get outside quick instead of waiting for me to come for you."

I need to remember that her worries and questions stem from being unsafe and unvalued in the past. These questions may seem silly to me, but they're a sign that her soul is unsettled, and deep down, she questions my unconditional love.

Truthfully, I could get offended. *Haven't I always been there? Haven't I tried and tried to show my love?* But the fact is, I haven't been nearly as faithful to my daughter as God has been to me. I do have bad moments—hard days when I question the goodness and faithfulness of God toward me. I get uptight about finances, upcoming work projects, and kids' wrong choices, forgetting that God has always provided and has always shown up for me and my kids.

It's easy to tell my daughter to trust, but it's harder sometimes to apply that advice to my own life. One of the reasons we don't have perfect peace is that we haven't created pockets of rest and renewal.

"All life requires a rhythm of rest," writes Wayne Muller in his book *Sabbath.* "We wake and we sleep. Day turns to night. The earth goes through seasons.... In our bodies, the heart perceptibly rests after each life-giving beat; the lungs rest between the exhale and the inhale."[1]

I do a pretty good job of working rest into my week. I make it a goal not to work on Sundays. I attempt to get enough sleep at night. But the same rhythm can apply to our souls, too. And as Scripture reminds us, soul rest comes when we turn to God, when we remember His goodness, and when we place our trust in Him for this day and all the days to come.

Turning to God sets our direction; looking to Him allows us to know where He's looking and where we should go. Remembering His goodness opens our heart to His work. Placing our trust in God reminds us to seek Him for wisdom. Resting in God seems to be doing nothing, but as our body stills, good work is getting done. It's like pausing at the start of a trip to turn on the GPS and enter the correct address. Doing so takes precious time—but it also saves time, gas, and the frustration that comes from heading the wrong way.

Have you ever tried to override what the GPS is telling you? I have. I've looked at the directions given and thought, "I know a faster way than that," only to discover road construction or rush hour traffic. Pausing, being open to direction, and seeking wisdom beyond ourselves is the first step.

A perfect example of not pausing—not trusting—happened twenty years ago on my first international trip. I was meeting up with friends in Europe, which meant I was traveling there and back alone. Things went smoothly on the way there, but on the trip home, I was to fly from Vienna through Paris and then to the U.S. I was warned that the Paris airport was hard to navigate, so I was already tense when my flight from Vienna was delayed.

To say that I was nervous as we landed in Paris at the time I was supposed to be departing was an understatement. I was a ball of nerves. It didn't help that nearly everyone on the plane appeared to be over the age of eighty and moved at the speed of molasses. I'm a polite person, but as everyone was departing that plane I wanted to shout, "Come on folks, MOVE!" When I finally got off the plane, my only hope was that the Paris to Atlanta flight was also delayed.

As I stepped into the terminal, I was confronted with a wall of gray hairs, and I soon discovered why. Up ahead was a man with a sign that read *Atlanta*. All the gray-hairs were lining up by the man, but I forged ahead. I did not want to stand around and wait for that crowd. I knew I could get to the gate sooner and hopefully catch the flight. So while dozens of others lined up by the sign, I hurried ahead.

My plan might have worked if I knew the layout of the Paris airport. Or if I read or spoke French. But I didn't, and I couldn't. Unlike most other places in Europe where I'd just traveled, in the Paris airport there were no signs in English to direct my way.

As I raced down the terminal, nothing made sense. The number system was wrong. The gate I was supposed to go to wasn't listed on any of the signs. I attempted to ask multiple airport attendants for help, but they did not speak English. (At least, not to me.) I rushed back to join that group of gray-hairs and the man with the sign, and they were gone, too. How had they left so quickly?

Desperate, I stood in the middle of the walkway calling out to everyone rushing by me in both directions, "Do you speak English? Do you speak English?" It was long past the time my plane was supposed to have departed, and I was completely lost.

After a few moments, a man in a business suit paused before me. "Yes, I speak English. How can I help you?"

I asked him about my gate, and he shook his head. "That gate is not in this terminal. It's in the second terminal. There is no way to get there except to leave this terminal and catch the bus to the other." He then glanced at my ticket and declared, "But you have no time for that!"

"Where do I find the bus to get me to the next terminal?" I asked, feeling my knees tremble.

Instead of answering me, he looked around, spotted an elevator and pointed to it. "Ah, come with me. I know a way."

I followed the man into the elevator, and he hit the bottom button. It was only he and I in the elevator when the doors opened to an underground parking garage.

He stepped out, and I froze. The place was empty. I found myself in the middle of a dimly lit underground parking lot with a stranger, without a soul around.

The man must have noticed my panic because he quickly stepped back inside the elevator and then pointed. "See that elevator on the other side of the garage? That goes to the next terminal. Take it to Floor Two and you'll be where you need to go."

I stepped out and the elevator doors closed behind me. Even though I was dragging luggage, I'm sure I clocked my personal best time running across that parking garage. I followed his directions and, sure enough, the doors opened to the correct place. My gate wasn't far from the elevator, and I was thankful to see that my flight had been delayed. I was also amused to see something else. All those gray hairs were waiting for me.

"Gray hair is a crown of splendor," we read in Proverbs 16:31 (NIV), and I understand why. Those men and women had learned over time to pause and pay attention. Instead of striking out on their own, they allowed themselves to be led. They stayed by the man with the sign who knew the way. They didn't waste all their time, energy, and emotions trying to find a better, faster way.

I'm pretty certain God sent a stranger in a business suit to help me. I was also pretty certain that my husband would never allow me to travel alone internationally again if he found out. I didn't tell John what had happened for over ten years. When I finally did confess, he wasn't happy. I assured him I'd learned my lesson: be patient and trust the one who knows the directions and will lead the way.

Also, it didn't occur to me at the time that the airline had actually sent the sign-holder to guide the passengers, knowing about the late plane. There's often more going on than we realize. It just takes standing still long enough to pay attention. It takes following the One who knows the way and allowing ourselves to be led. We can follow God to find our refuge. We can also seek Him to better understand ourselves—and to understand what misconceptions we have that are sending us down wrong paths.

Discovering and Becoming

One thing we often forget is that we choose who we become. Before I was an accomplished writer, I was someone who set aside time each day to write. For many years, the majority of my writing consisted of small devotional thoughts that I put together for an email prayer/praise report. My audience was fifteen writer friends. They'd send me their updates, I'd compile them into an email, add a devotional thought, and send them out. Looking back, it's clear that I was building community, learning to depend on God, and giving time and diligence to my writing. I was becoming a friend, a person of prayer, and a writer, even when I didn't realize it.

There is a downside for those of us who discover the places where we are uniquely talented and begin to bloom. Finding joy in our work, it's easy to take our gazes off the One who gifted us with our talents. Instead, we focus on the object of our creation and even ourselves as creative people.

This happened when I first began writing. When a friend mentioned she was working on a novel, something zinged inside my heart. As someone who loved reading, at that moment I knew that was what I'd been called to do. Yet in the years that have followed, there has been a tug-of-war within my heart. I've discovered what I love, and this small love has taken my attention off the big love of God at times.

After finding some level of success, it becomes easier to believe it's all about me: my talents, my ideas, my work ethic. In times of struggle, I'm reminded that all I do is because of God.

At another level, my writing career also has me battling my two core issues on a near-daily basis: belonging/acceptance and approval. Looking back at myself as a child, I can see how much I wanted to be seen, to be accepted and praised. Sadly, broken people raise broken people, and more often than not, those needs went unmet. During my teen years, this led me to unhealthy relationships with guys—but I can also see how this plays out in my writing life.

I come up with ideas that need to be accepted by publishers first and readers later. Then, these readers have the opportunity to rate me on my work. It's very easy for me to fix my attention on the numbers: sales figures and star ratings. And there have been times when I thought these things really don't matter. The truth was they didn't matter because I found myself on the bestseller's list and with a majority of five-star ratings.

I only figured out that I still struggled with this when, during the pandemic, I started doing virtual tours through HeyGo.com. I joined an international network of tour guides who provided free tours of their part of the world in exchange for tips. Even though I wasn't a professional tour guide, I do love my "world"—both where I live in Little Rock, Arkansas, and my own "world" of researching, writing, and storytelling. I decided to give tours on both.

As a public speaker, I know how to pull together stories and ideas. I researched how to give LIVE presentations, eager to connect with viewers from all over the world. But my first three tours had to be canceled due to an arctic storm that dumped snow on Little Rock, shutting down our city. Even though I had no control, I felt like I'd failed before I even got started.

Then, when I started giving tours, the ratings were like a punch to my gut. While most were positive, there were some people who gave me one-star ratings. Some people thought I was too chatty. Others thought one of my cooking tours was especially disjointed and disorganized. (Looking back, I can see that it was!)

For someone used to getting applause and approval, this was tough. My heart was crushed, and again my eyes turned away from the purpose (to connect with an international community, to build friendships, and to offer hope) and instead to the numbers and ratings.

I wish I could say that I brushed it off, but it was a battle. I conversed with others about how unfair it was for people to leave harsh reviews when we were offering our tours for free. I moped around the house, and I even found myself short-tempered with my family. It wasn't until my family wanted to know what was wrong that I realized these ratings had shot arrows at my core needs for belonging, acceptance, and approval. Let me tell you, my heart was not happy—anything but.

Yet I've learned that instead of allowing these feelings of unworthiness to take root, I needed to battle them. I did this by going before God in prayer. In tears, I poured out my feelings. I also took time to think back on other times I felt unseen and unappreciated. I thought about growing up in a house where I had learned that to be considered good, I had to make people happy.

I thought about not making the cheerleading team in junior high, then making it in high school but always feeling like I was the least pretty and least popular one in the group. I thought about wanting the attention of boys and not getting it—then getting it and realizing that the love of high school boyfriends would never fill the empty places inside my heart.

As I thought about these things, I asked Jesus to bring healing. I asked Him to search my heart and touch the places where pain from the past made these silly star ratings from the present sting so much. I also thanked Him for allowing me to get such bad reviews. I needed to be reminded that I'm not always going to get everything right the first time. I also had to feel the pain deep in my heart to discover the places that I still needed to allow Jesus inside to work.

As I was crying, I prayed, "Search me, O God, and know my heart; test me and know my anxious thoughts. Point out anything in me that offends you, and lead me along the path of everlasting life." (Psalm 139:23–24)

When I first memorized this verse in 2005, it was in the New King James Version, which uses the term "wicked way" instead of "that offends you." At the time, I pictured God pointing out my sins, especially sins of the past that I still clung to. This brought a lot of healing, which I really needed.

Then, as I was praying this scripture again, I felt God's gentle whisper saying, "Maybe some of the offensive lies planted in your heart weren't placed there by you." My head popped up, and my mind started traveling down a new path. Surely there were lies in my heart that came from others' words. Maybe I not only needed to ask God to search me for sins, but I also needed to ask Him to search my heart for lies and mistruths that had found their way deep inside me—things that no longer needed to be there.

When I looked up "wicked way," I discovered the Hebrew word may mean "way of sorrow" such as that of a woman in labor[2] or the harsh labor the Egyptians inflicted on the Israelite slaves.

I started to see that the things that offend God are also the things that have caused me great pain and kept me in bondage. Feeling the clear ache inside, I realized that even though I've learned to maneuver around those tender, lacerated spots, they are still there. More than that, too often I've worked and worked to answer the master who demands that I work for numbers and approval instead of walking in step with God. What a revelation!

Once I began discovering these lies I had believed about myself, I next started looking toward God's truths. Who was I really? Who did God design me to be? How could I connect with God in the ways He's uniquely designed for me?

Fully Ourselves

God not only knows the way we are to go, He knows us. He knows our flaws, yet He knows our beauty, too. God knows how He designed us, and how our souls can best connect with Him. It's important to pause and discover how He sees us.

"One of the greatest victories we can win for our heavenly father is to refuse to live in insecurity," writes author Holley Gerth.

True humility—the kind Jesus demonstrated—is fully knowing who we really are and then choosing to love

and serve from that place. And holy confidence is an act
of war against the enemy of our hearts. We are significant threats when we understand we have valuable gifts
within us. Because then we actually dare to offer them.[3]

What are some of your gifts that God desires to breathe new
life into? What renews and rejuvenates your heart? Many of us have
creative endeavors we enjoy. We often call these "hobbies," and we
only take time for them after we get our work done. Yet we must
remember that we were created in God's likeness. We were designed
to be creative beings. Our soul is nourished when we take time for
creativity and reflection. We can foster intimacy with God when
we enjoy the interests, gifts, and talents He has given us. We find
great joy for our souls when we fully become who God created us
to be.

We get so used to reacting, we don't take time to act—to be
intentional. To explore our emotions and express ourselves. To be
creative and create. We can best feed our souls by discovering the
unique ways we connect with God.

My friend, Dr. Kathy Koch, is a genius when it comes to understanding our unique intelligence. She has written about this in
numerous books, including 8 Great Smarts: Discover and Nurture
Your Child's Intelligences. Kathy has applied what she's learned to
how we relate to God, and she's given me permission to share it in
this book. Kathy recognizes a person's relationship with God is
influenced by many things and not just their multiple intelligences.
Still, I believe all of us can look at these descriptions and understand
how we can uniquely relate to God, thus nurturing our souls.

1. Word Smart. We enjoy using more than one translation of
the Bible and looking words up in the original languages of Hebrew

and Greek to further unpack their meanings. Knowing the names of God and Christ will enrich our understanding. We probably enjoy reading and studying the Bible more than others might and learn rather easily from sermons and talk radio. We probably like teaching or explaining what we know. God will probably primarily communicate to us through His Word. We may serve by teaching, writing newsletters, proofreading, and being effective with our words.

2. Logic Smart. We like looking up cross references and maybe using commentaries. We need safe people to answer our questions. We need things to think about, things that teach us well and don't bore us. Our knowledge of God may be most important to us. Because we want things to make sense, we benefit from seeing consistency in the four gospels and across the Bible. We may benefit from connecting with others and having the freedom to discuss our faith. We may doubt more, be resistant to new revelations, and need more assurance than others that our conversion experience was real.

3. Picture Smart. We visualize as we read Scripture and listen to sermons. We feel honored when people ask us what we see. Some of us will have detailed descriptions of God Himself and can even imagine the inside of a fish's stomach. After Sunday school or church, we enjoy having people ask us if God showed us anything rather than just asking us what we learned. We will prefer churches with banners, art, or displays, and we may doodle or sketch during sermons and seminars. God may *show* us what to do rather than, or in addition to, telling us. We may serve by decorating, designing, or drawing.

4. Music Smart. We may enjoy studying passages that mention music and dance. We may want to understand how worship and music were used during Old Testament times. We may enjoy the

poetry of the Psalms. Worship may be our favorite part of a church service, and we may be on the worship team. We may feel closest to God during worship and have no trouble worshipping alone. We'll benefit if music is used in family devotions. God may speak to us through it. We may enjoy studying the lyrics of great hymns and contemporary songs and learning about the composers.

5. Body Smart. We may struggle in church if we have to sit still too long. Activities in youth group and church-camp settings may be our favorites. We may worship with hands raised and may prefer to clap and sway or dance to the music. We may see fitness and nutrition as acts of worship. We may enjoy Bible verses about the body and relate well to analogies about the body. We may feel God's presence and know what to do because we feel it in our gut. We may need to *feel* close to God. We can serve by being on a drama team, setting things up, and doing other physical tasks.

6. Nature Smart. We feel closest to God when outside. For some, that looks like being in the mountains and for others, it's being by the ocean. We want churches to have windows and plants. We may relate well to God as Creator and enjoy studying about creation. We may debate those who believe in evolution. We also may enjoy and benefit from passages that describe things of nature— about Noah and Jonah and many Psalms. If you want to talk with us about God, we might engage more if we're outside. We can serve by planting and tending to gardens and taking care of sanctuary plants and holiday flowers.

7. People Smart. We may enjoy learning about Jesus's interactions with people and the one-anothers of the New Testament. We may be the ones who love people best and need to connect one-on-one with the pastor in order to learn the most. We may enjoy special events, fellowships, and committees. We may enjoy and learn well

in interactive small groups. It may be hard for us to be quiet for long periods. We may prioritize our relationship with God over our knowledge of God. Praying may be a strength. We may serve through hospitality and leading.

8. Self Smart. Because we like thinking alone and need quietness and time to process, we may have a hard time with church. We may not join small groups because of their quick pace and because we usually don't enjoy sharing what we know. We may enjoy journaling our thoughts in private. We may meet God in quiet and private places and have many profound thoughts. We may go on our own spiritual retreats, but not church retreats with many other people. We may be prayer warriors and enjoy serving behind the scenes.

Did you see yourself in these smarts? I highly recommend getting Dr. Kathy Koch's books and exploring these intelligences more. Understanding how you better connect with God can also help you discover ways to nurture your soul and become heart happy.

Let's End with the Basics

When all else fails, remember it's important to go back to the basics. Caring for your soul also means caring for yourself. We need to make sure we get enough sleep. We need to eat what is healthy. We need to enjoy the people in our lives. We need to discover where we find joy.

One of the basic things I've done to care for my soul has been discovering my love of watercolor painting and drawing. When the pressures of the last year pressed down, I decided to pick up a paintbrush.

Growing up, I loved to draw. I can remember at a very young age illustrating the world around me. My grandmother would always look at my work and tell me that someday I was going to have a line of greeting cards. I'd forgotten that until I took time to pause.

Remembering how drawing had brought me joy, I ordered pencils, pens, and paper. Thinking about how I'd always wanted to learn how to watercolor paint, I ordered painting supplies, too. I'd gotten to this place because I took time to consider who I was and who God created me to be.

What about you? Consider what you loved to do when you were young. If you could take up a hobby, what would it be? Making time for that may be just what your soul needs.

I sat down to paint because I needed to do something for me, to discover a bit of joy. What has been the result? Around my bedroom, I have piles of papers covered with my art. I have created greeting cards, and they are for sale on my website. And if you look at the cover of this book...yes, that's my art too.

More than that, I've found freedom. I've learned that my soul needs time to breathe, just as it needs time with God. Art allows me to do that. My heart is happy in numerous ways, and even though there are hard things in my life, I feel closer to God than ever before.

God did not welcome us into His Kingdom to have more workers available to impact the world, but so we could be *His* children in a loving relationship with *Him* for eternity. Remembering this makes me think of my children, both biological and adopted. John and I didn't grow our family to get out of doing chores ourselves (what a joke, right?) but because our hearts' desire was for the special kinship that comes when we call someone "son" or "daughter." When each of us can truly grasp this, our strivings will cease. In Jesus's arms, we will discover the life we were meant to live and the love our hearts long for.

One hymn that speaks to these truths was a favorite of missionary Hudson Taylor, founder of China Inland Mission. This is my favorite verse of "Jesus, I Am Resting" by Jean S. Pigott, written in 1876:

> Ever lift Thy face upon me
> As I work and wait for Thee;
> Resting 'neath Thy smile, Lord Jesus,
> Earth's dark shadows flee.
> Brightness of my Father's glory,
> Sunshine of my Father's face,
> Keep me ever trusting, resting,
> Fill me with Thy grace.

Today, there is no greater work for us than to turn our attention to Jesus's face upon us. Pause and imagine His smile, and as you do, the dark shadows of striving and comparison will be pushed out by the light of His face. Can you imagine how He lights up when we're enjoying the things He specifically created us to enjoy?

I'm sharing this message not only for you, but for myself. Since all of us are prone to be our own worst enemies, let us also make a habit of turning to Jesus and allowing His faithfulness to be a shield and a wall of protection. May we each find refuge in His everlasting care today. May we allow ourselves to use our unique gifts to connect with Him. And may we truly discover how heart happy changes everything, because of Him.

Digging Deeper

For years, I constructed vision boards with the teen moms in our support group, but I'd walk away discouraged. My idea was that these young moms would consider reachable goals for the years ahead and cut out images to inspire them when times got hard—things like a photo of a high school graduate, a person exercising, or a mom on the floor playing with her baby. Instead, from the stack of magazines I'd brought in, they would cut out pictures of the nicest cars, the poshest apartments, and the blingiest jewelry one could imagine.

As a leader, I quickly saw their "vision" of the things of this world had nothing to do with reality. Even though these young women lived in the inner city and worked to survive day to day, they'd picked up on what the world believes is important. Yet if any of us have learned anything during the last few years, it's that what the world considers important can be quickly stripped away. It's what we have left—us and God—that matters.

The possessions we prize will become useless or unattainable. Designer gowns and trendy clothes fall out of style. Exclusive restaurants close. Blowouts and manicures do not care for the soul. And as we all found out in 2020, vacations can be canceled, theme parks closed down, and shopping malls boarded up. And through this, we discover what truly matters—we enjoy time with our families. We reconnect with old friends. Hobbies are resurrected. We enjoy activities we didn't dare take time for before. We discover life without rush, and our ideas of what is "important" change.

When all the external finds itself on shaky ground, God remains: steady, strong, ever-present. When we care for our souls, we find new life and new hope. We see that heart happy is something we can attain because of Jesus. We look to Him and look to the future, knowing that we are changed and we can make a hope-filled journey together.

Your Turn

I'm so thankful that each of us can go before God individually. Take time to ponder these questions next time you do. As you are still before Him, ask Him where your peace and heart happiness can be found.

1. God, where are You working? What are the open doors?
2. What is breathing life into me right now? What out-pouring (something I do) is also filling me up (inpouring) with You?
3. What are people asking me for? How can I best love and serve out of my natural talents?
4. What truth are You speaking into my heart?
5. What have You uniquely created me to do that I need to make time for? How can I be creative with You by my side?

5 Minutes to Connect

Read over the "8 Smarts" again as described by Dr. Kathy Koch. Sit before God and ask Him to show you who He created you to be. Then create a list of things you can do to connect with Him on a more regular basis according to your smarts.

Notes

Chapter One

1. George Müller, *Autobiography of George Müller: A Million and a Half in Answer to Prayer* (Vestavia Hills, Alabama: Solid Ground Christian Books, 2004), 693.
2. "Soul Nourishment First," GeorgeMuller.org, July 7, 2016, https://www.georgemuller.org/devotional/soul-nourishment-first.html.
3. Ibid.
4. Linda Cochrane, *Forgiven and Set Free: A Post-Abortion Bible Study for Women* (Ada, Michigan: Baker Books, 2015).
5. Andrew Farley and Tim Chalas, *The Perfect You: God's Invitation to Live from the Heart* (Washington, D.C.: Salem Books, 2021), 58–59.

Chapter Three

1. Paul David Tripp, "March 7," *New Morning Mercies* (Wheaton, Illinois: Crossway Books, 2014).
2. "The 3 Parts of Man—Spirit, Soul, and Body," *Bibles for America* blog, June 1, 2021, https://blog.biblesforamerica.org/the-three-parts-of-man-spirit-soul-and-body.html.
3. "Soul Nourishment First," GeorgeMuller.org, July 7, 2016, https://www.georgemuller.org/devotional/soul-nourishment-first.html.
4. Ibid.
5. Brennan Manning et al., *ABBA's Child: The Cry of the Heart for Intimate Belonging* (Colorado Springs: NavPress, 2015), 24.
6. John Eldredge, *Wild at Heart Field Manual: A Personal Guide to Discovering the Secret of Your Masculine Soul* (Nashville: Thomas Nelson Publishers, 2002), 124.

Chapter Four

1. Andrew Farley and Tim Chalas, *The Perfect You: God's Invitation to Live from the Heart* (Washington, D.C.: Salem Books, 2021), 124.
2. Paul David Tripp, "January 14," *New Morning Mercies* (Wheaton, Illinois: Crossway Books, 2014).

Chapter Five

1. "Strong's Hebrew: 1288. חָרַב (Barak)–to Kneel, Bless," Bible Hub, https://biblehub.com/hebrew/1288.htm.
2. "Strong's Hebrew: 835. יְאִשֶׁר (Esher)–Happiness, Blessedness," Bible Hub, https://biblehub.com/hebrew/835.htm.
3. "Strong's Hebrew: 833. וֹאִשַׁר (Ashar)–to Go Straight, Go on, Advance," Bible Hub, https://biblehub.com/hebrew/833.htm.
4. "Barnes' Notes: Psalm 1:1 'Blessed is the man that walketh not in the counsel of the ungodly, nor standeth in the way of sinners, nor sitteth in the seat of the scornful,'" Bible Hub, https://biblehub.com/commentaries/barnes/psalms/1.htm.
5. Jeff Benner, "Studies in the Psalms: Psalm 1," Ancient Hebrew Research Center, https://www.ancient-hebrew.org/psalms/studies-in-the-psalms-psalm-1.htm.
6. Randy C. Alcorn, *Money, Possessions, and Eternity* (Wheaton, Illinois: Tyndale House Publishers, 2003), 33.
7. Augustine et al., *Sermons (306-340A) on the Saints* (Hyde Park, New York: New City Press, 1994), 18.
8. Charles Spurgeon, *The Complete Works of C. H. Spurgeon, Volume 75* (Fort Collins, Colorado: Delmarva Publications, Inc., 2015).
9. Randy C. Alcorn, *Does God Want Us to Be Happy?: The Case for Biblical Happiness* (Carol Stream, Illinois: Tyndale, 2019), 4.

10. "Acts 17, Ellicott's Commentary for English Readers," Bible Hub, https://biblehub.com/commentaries/ellicott/acts/17.htm.

11. Paul David Tripp, "February 18," *New Morning Mercies* (Wheaton, Illinois: Crossway Books, 2014).

12. Agnes Heller, "The Power of Shame," *Dialectical Anthropology* 6, no. 3 (1982): 215–28, http://www.jstor.org/stable/29790037.

Chapter Six

1. "Soul Nourishment First," GeorgeMuller.org, July 7, 2016, https://www.georgemuller.org/devotional/soul-nourishment-first.html.

2. Ibid.

3. Dutch Sheets, *Intercessory Prayer: How Prayer Really Works* (Minneapolis: Bethany House, 2016), 182.

4. Henry T. Blackaby et al., *Experiencing God: Knowing and Doing the Will of God* (Nashville: LifeWay Press, 2007), 33.

5. Ibid.

6. Pete Scazzero, *Emotionally Healthy Spirituality, Unleash the Power of Life in Christ* (Nashville: Thomas Nelson, 2006), 129.

7. *Church Harmonies, New and Old, A Book of Spiritual Song for Christian Worshippers* (Palala Press, 1913), 300.

8. Don Lynch and Ken Marschall, *Titanic: An Illustrated History* 2nd ed. (London: Hodder & Stoughton, 1997), 77.

9. Corrie ten Boom, *The Hiding Place* (New York: Bantam Books, 1974), 190.

10. David G. Benner, *Care of Souls: Revisioning Christian Nurture and Counsel* (Grand Rapids, Michigan: Baker Books, 2004), 26.

11. The tune is anonymous; the words are by John Newton, 1725–1807.

Chapter Seven

1. David G. Benner, *Care of Souls: Revisioning Christian Nurture and Counsel* (Grand Rapids, Michigan: Baker Books, 2004), 21–22.
2. Kristy Cambron, *Verse Mapping Bible Study Journal* (Nashville: Thomas Nelson, 2021), 5.
3. Paul David Tripp, "February 23," *New Morning Mercies* (Wheaton, Illinois: Crossway Books, 2014).
4. Bethany Dearborn Hiser, *From Burned Out to Beloved: Soul Care for Wounded Healers* (Downers Grove, Illinois: IVP Books, 2020), 20.
5. Ibid., 18.

Chapter Eight

1. Jill Suttie, "Does Self-Compassion Make You Compassionate toward Others?" Greater Good Science Center, https://greatergood.berkeley.edu/article/item/does_self_compassion_make_you_compassionate_toward_others.
2. Bethany Dearborn Hiser, *From Burned Out to Beloved: Soul Care for Wounded Healers* (Downers Grove, Illinois: IVP Books, 2020), 6.
3. Rick and Forrest Hanson, *Resilient: How to Grow an Unshakable Core of Calm, Strength, and Happiness* (New York: Harmony Books, 2018), 10.

Chapter Nine

1. Tony Schwartz, "The Importance of Naming Your Emotions," *New York Times*, April 3, 2015, https://www.nytimes.com/2015/04/04/business/dealbook/the-importance-of-naming-your-emotions.html.
2. Paul David Tripp, "March 1," *New Morning Mercies* (Wheaton, Illinois: Crossway Books, 2014).

3. Rick and Forrest Hanson, *Resilient: How to Grow an Unshakable Core of Calm, Strength, and Happiness* (New York: Harmony Books, 2018), 1.

4. "Building Your Resilience," American Psychological Association, last modified February 1, 2020, https://www.apa.org/topics/resilience.

Chapter Ten

1. Wayne Sabler, *Sabbath: Finding Rest, Renewal, and Delight in Our Busy Lives* (New York: Bantam Books, 2000), 1.

2. Psalm 139:24, "See If There Is Any Offensive Way in Me; Lead Me in the Way Everlasting," Bible Hub, https://biblehub.com/psalms/139-24.htm.

3. Holley Gerth, *Strong, Brave, Loved: Empowering Reminders of Who You Really Are* (Ada, Michigan: Revell, 2019), 12.